DISCOURSE ON METHOD
AND
MEDITATIONS

René Descartes

Translated by
Elizabeth S. Haldane and G. R. T. Ross

Pascals wager

	God	no god
Believe	Heaven	no worse off - no hell
not believe	Hell	no worse off - no hell

Best bet is to believe

god by nature is definitely perfect b/c everyone/a

DOVER PUBLICATIONS, INC.
Mineola, New York

DOVER PHILOSOPHICAL CLASSICS

Copyright

Bibliographical Note

This Dover edition, first published in 2003, is an unabridged republication of the sections "Discourse on the Method of Rightly Conducting the
Reason" and "Meditations on First Philosophy" from the 1955 Dover edition of *The Philosophical Works of Descartes* (Volume 1). The 1955 Dover
edition was an unabridged republication of the 1931 edition of the work,
published through special arrangement with Cambridge University Press;
the 1931 edition was a corrected reprint of the 1911 Cambridge University
Press first edition. A new introductory Note has been specially prepared
for the present edition.

Library of Congress Cataloging-in-Publication Data

Descartes, René, 1596–1650.
    [Discours de la méthode. English]
    Discourse on method ; and, Meditations / René Descartes ; translated
by Elizabeth S. Haldane and G.R.T. Ross.
        p. cm. — (Dover philosophical classics)
    ISBN 0-486-43252-1 (pbk.)
        1. Methodology. 2. Knowledge, Theory of. 3. Science—Methodology.
4. First philosophy. I. Title: Discourse on method ; and, Meditations. II.
Haldane, Elizabeth Sanderson, 1862–1937. III. Ross, G. R. T. (George
Robert Thomson) IV. Descartes, René, 1596–1650. Meditationes de prima
philosophia. English. V. Title: Meditations. VI. Title. VII. Series.

B1848.E5H35 2003
194—dc22

                                                            2003060054

Manufactured in the United States of America
Dover Publications, Inc., 31 East 2nd Street, Mineola, N.Y. 11501

what makes us human is our <u>reason</u>

Reason is the <u>mind</u>
                <u>consciousness</u>
        mind is the seed of the soul

what is consciousness?

human - animal divide

PUBLISHER'S NOTE

Elizabeth S. Haldane and G. R. T. Ross, the translators of the 1911 edition of *The Philosophical Works of Descartes*, based their text on a new edition of Descartes' works [*Oeuvres de Descartes*] that was prepared by Charles Adam and Paul Tannery and published by Léopold Cerf, Paris (1897–1913).

The first edition of *Meditations on First Philosophy* was published in Latin by Michael Soly, Paris, in 1641. A second edition, published in 1642 in Amsterdam by Louis Elzevir, was used by Adam and Tannery in their *Oeuvres de Descartes*. The *Discourse on the Method of Rightly Conducting the Reason*, Descartes' first published work (published anonymously), was initially brought out by Jan Maire, Leiden, in 1637. The Latin version of the original French text was prepared by Étienne de Courcelles and published by Louis Elzevir, Amsterdam, in 1644.

Descartes believed -
        mind) rational
        soul } "made in
        Reason) God's image'
    mind makes us human.

Dualism (cartesian)
    human - animal split

iii

If I can prove any object exists independent of me, then a world an objective must.

Real fear to be alone

Trademark Argument - god planted the idea of himself in our own heads

CONTENTS

Cogito ergo sum -
   I think; therefore I am

- Freewill defense human behavior
- god has a cosmic perspective - we cant understand.
- god isnt finished yet
- god isnt omni-

DISCOURSE ON METHOD

DISCOURSE ON THE METHOD OF RIGHTLY CONDUCTING THE REASON AND SEEKING FOR TRUTH IN THE SCIENCES.

If this Discourse appears too long to be read all at once, it may be separated into six portions. And in the first there will be found various considerations respecting the sciences; in the second, the principal rules regarding the Method which the author has sought out; while in the third are some of the rules of morality which he has derived from this Method. In the fourth are the reasons by which he proves the existence of God and of the human soul, which form the foundation of his Metaphysic. In the fifth, the order of the questions regarding physics which he has investigated, and particularly the explanation of the movement of the heart, and of some other difficulties which pertain to medicine, as also the difference between the soul of man and that of the brutes. And in the last part the questions raised relate to those matters which the author believes to be requisite in order to advance further in the investigation of nature, in addition to the reasons that caused him to write.

PART I.

Good sense is of all things in the world the most equally distributed, for everybody thinks himself so abundantly provided with it, that even those most difficult to please in all other matters do not commonly desire more of it than they already possess. It is unlikely that this is an error on their part; it seems rather to be evidence in support of the view that the power of forming a good judgment and of distinguishing the true from the false, which is properly speaking what is called Good sense or Reason, is by nature equal in all men. Hence too it will show that the diversity of our opinions does not proceed from some men being more rational than others, but solely from the fact that our thoughts pass through diverse channels and the same objects are not considered by all. For to be possessed of good mental powers is not sufficient; the principal matter is to apply them well. The greatest minds are capable of the greatest vices as well as of the greatest virtues, and those who proceed very slowly may, provided they always follow the straight road, really advance much faster than those who, though they run, forsake it.

For myself I have never ventured to presume that my mind was in any way more perfect than that of the ordinary man; I have even longed to possess thought as quick, or an imagination as accurate and distinct, or a memory as comprehensive or ready, as some others. And besides these I do not know any other qualities that make for the perfection of the human mind. For as to reason or sense, inasmuch as it is the only thing that constitutes us men and distinguishes us from the brutes, I would fain believe that it is to be found complete in each individual, and in this I follow the common opinion of the philosophers, who say that the question of more or less occurs only in the sphere of the *accidents* and does not affect the *forms* or natures of the *individuals* in the same *species*.

But I shall not hesitate to say that I have had great good fortune from my youth up, in lighting upon and pursuing certain paths which have conducted me to considerations and maxims from which I have formed a Method, by whose assistance it appears to me I have the means of gradually increasing my knowledge and of little by little raising it to the highest possible point which the mediocrity of my talents and the brief duration of my life can permit me to reach. For I have already reaped from it fruits of such a nature that, even though I always try in the judgments I make on myself to lean to the side of self-depreciation rather than to that of arrogance, and though, looking with the eye of a philosopher on the diverse actions and enterprises of all mankind, I find scarcely any which do not seem to me vain and useless, I do not cease to receive extreme satisfaction in the progress which I seem to have already made in the search after truth, and to form such hopes for the future as to venture to believe that, if amongst the occupations of men, simply as men, there is some one in particular that is excellent and important, that is the one which I have selected.

It must always be recollected, however, that possibly I deceive myself, and that what I take to be gold and diamonds is perhaps no more than copper and glass. I know how subject we are to delusion in whatever touches ourselves, and also how much the judgments of our friends ought to be suspected when they are in our favour. But in this Discourse I shall be very happy to show the paths I have followed, and to set forth my life as in a picture, so that everyone may judge of it for himself; and thus in learning from the common talk what are the opinions which are held of it, a new means of obtaining self-instruction will be reached, which I shall add to those which I have been in the habit of using.

Thus my design is not here to teach the Method which everyone should follow in order to promote the good conduct of his Reason, but only to show in what manner I have endeavoured to conduct my own. Those who set about giving precepts must esteem themselves more skilful than those to whom they advance them, and if they fall short in the smallest matter they must of course take the blame for it. But regarding this Treatise simply as a history, or, if you prefer it, a fable in which, amongst certain things which may be imitated, there are possibly others also which it would not be right to follow, I hope that it will be of use to some without being hurtful to any, and that all will thank me for my frankness.

I have been nourished on letters since my childhood, and since I was given to believe that by their means a clear and certain knowledge could be obtained of all that is useful in life, I had an extreme desire to acquire instruction. But so soon as I had achieved the entire course of study at the close of which one is usually received into the ranks of the learned, I entirely changed my opinion. For I found myself embarrassed with so many doubts and errors that it seemed to me that the effort to instruct myself had no effect other than the increasing discovery of my own ignorance. And yet I was studying at one of the most celebrated Schools in Europe, where I thought that there must be men of learning if they were to be found anywhere in the world. I learned there all that others learned; and not being satisfied with the sciences that we were taught, I even read through all the books which fell into my hands, treating of what is considered most curious and rare. Along with this I knew the judgments that others had formed of me, and I did not feel that I was esteemed inferior to my fellow-students, although there were amongst them some destined to fill the places of our masters. And finally our century seemed to me as flourishing, and as fertile in great minds, as any which had preceded. And this made me take the liberty of judging all others by myself and of coming to the conclusion that there was no learning in the world such as I was formerly led to believe it to be.

I did not omit, however, always to hold in esteem those exercises which are the occupation of the Schools. I knew that the Languages which one learns there are essential for the understanding of all ancient literature; that fables with their charm stimulate the mind and histories of memorable deeds exalt it; and that, when read with discretion, these books assist in forming a sound judgment. I was aware that the reading of all good books is indeed like a conversation with the noblest men of past centuries who were the authors of them, nay a carefully studied conversation, in which they reveal to us none but the best of their thoughts. I deemed Eloquence to have a power and beauty beyond compare; that Poesy has most ravishing delicacy and sweetness; that in Mathematics there are the subtlest discoveries and inventions which may accomplish much, both in satisfying the curious, and in furthering all the arts, and in diminishing man's labour; that those writings that deal with Morals contain much that is instructive, and many exhortations to virtue which are most useful; that Theology points out the way to Heaven; that Philosophy teaches us to speak with an appearance of truth on all things, and causes us to be admired by the less learned; that Jurisprudence, Medicine and all other sciences bring honour and riches to those who cultivate them; and finally that it is good to have examined all things, even those most full of superstition and falsehood, in order that we may know their just value, and avoid being deceived by them.

But I considered that I had already given sufficient time to languages and likewise even to the reading of the literature of the ancients, both their histories and their fables. For to converse with those of other centuries is almost the same thing as to travel. It is good to know something of the customs of different peoples in order to judge more sanely of our own, and not to think that everything of a fashion not ours is absurd and contrary to reason, as do those who have seen nothing. But when one employs too much time in travelling, one becomes a stranger in one's own country, and when one is too curious about things which were practised in past centuries, one is usually very ignorant about those which are practised in our own time. Besides, fables make one imagine many events possible which in reality are not so, and even the most accurate of histories, if they do not exactly misrepresent or exaggerate the value of things in order to render them more worthy of being read, at least omit in them all the circumstances which are basest and least notable ; and from this fact it follows that what is retained is not portrayed as it really is, and that those who regulate their conduct by examples which they derive from such a source, are liable to fall into the extravagances of the knights-errant of Romance, and form projects beyond their power of performance.

I esteemed Eloquence most highly and I was enamoured of Poesy, but I thought that both were gifts of the mind rather than fruits of study. Those who have the strongest power of reasoning, and who most skilfully arrange their thoughts in order to render them clear and intelligible, have the best power of persuasion even if they can but speak the language of Lower Brittany and have never learned Rhetoric. And those who have the most delightful original ideas and who know how to express them with the maximum of style and suavity, would not fail to be the best poets even if the art of Poetry were unknown to them.

Most of all was I delighted with Mathematics because of the certainty of its demonstrations and the evidence of its reasoning ; but I did not yet understand its true use, and, believing that it was of service only in the mechanical arts, I was astonished that, seeing how firm and solid was its basis, no loftier edifice had been reared thereupon. On the other hand I compared the works of the ancient pagans which deal with Morals to palaces most superb and magnificent, which are yet built on sand and mud alone. They praise the virtues most highly and show them to be more worthy of being prized than anything else in the world, but they do not sufficiently teach us to become acquainted with them, and often that which is called by a fine name is nothing but insensibility, or pride, or despair, or parricide.

I honoured our Theology and aspired as much as anyone to reach to heaven, but having learned to regard it as a most highly assured fact that the road is not less open to the most ignorant than to the most learned, and that the revealed truths which conduct thither are quite above our intelligence, I should not have dared to submit them to the feebleness of my reasonings ; and I thought that, in order to undertake to examine them and succeed in so doing, it was necessary to have some extraordinary assistance from above and to be more than a mere man.

I shall not say anything about Philosophy, but that, seeing that it has been cultivated for many centuries by the best minds that have ever lived, and that nevertheless no single thing is to be found in it which is not subject of dispute, and in consequence which is not dubious, I had not enough presumption to hope to fare better there than other men had done. And also, considering how many conflicting opinions there may be regarding the self-same matter, all supported by learned people, while there can never be more than one which is true, I esteemed as well-nigh false all that only went as far as being probable.

Then as to the other sciences, inasmuch as they derive their principles from Philosophy, I judged that one could have built nothing solid on foundations so far from firm. And neither the honour nor the promised gain was sufficient to persuade me to cultivate them, for, thanks be to God, I did not find myself in a condition which obliged me to make a merchandise of science for the improvement of my fortune; and, although I did not pretend to scorn all glory like the Cynics, I yet had very small esteem for what I could not hope to acquire, excepting through fictitious titles. And, finally, as to false doctrines, I thought that I already knew well enough what they were worth to be subject to deception neither by the promises of an alchemist, the predictions of an astrologer, the impostures of a magician, the artifices or the empty boastings of any of those who make a profession of knowing that of which they are ignorant.

This is why, as soon as age permitted me to emerge from the control of my tutors, I entirely quitted the study of letters. And resolving to seek no other science than that which could be found in myself, or at least in the great book of the world, I employed the rest of my youth in travel, in seeing courts and armies, in intercourse with men of diverse temperaments and conditions, in collecting varied experiences, in proving myself in the various predicaments in which I was placed by fortune, and under all circumstances bringing my mind to bear on the things which came before it, so that I might derive some profit from my experience. For it seemed to me that I might meet with much more truth in the reasonings that each man makes on the matters that specially concern him, and the issue of which would very soon punish him if he made a wrong judgment, than in the case of those made by a man of letters in his study touching speculations which lead to no result, and which bring about no other consequences to himself excepting that he will be all the more vain the more they are removed from common sense, since in this case it proves him to have employed so much the more ingenuity and skill in trying to make them seem probable. And I always had an excessive desire to learn to distinguish the true from the false, in order to see clearly in my actions and to walk with confidence in this life.

It is true that while I only considered the manners of other men I found in them nothing to give me settled convictions; and I remarked in them almost as much diversity as I had formerly seen in the opinions of philosophers. So much was this the case that the greatest profit which I derived from their study was that, in seeing many things which, although they seem to us very extravagant and ridiculous, were yet commonly received and approved by other great nations, I learned to believe nothing too certainly of which I had only been convinced by example and custom. Thus little by little I was delivered from many errors which might have obscured our natural vision and rendered us less capable of listening to Reason. But after I had employed several years in thus studying the book of the world and trying to acquire some experience, I one day formed the resolution of also making myself an object of study and of employing all the strength of my mind in choosing the road I should follow. This succeeded much better, it appeared to me, than if I had never departed either from my country or my books.

PART II.

I was then in Germany, to which country I had been attracted by the wars which are not yet at an end. And as I was returning from the coronation of the Emperor to join the army, the setting in of winter detained me in a quarter where, since I found no society to divert me, while fortunately I had also no cares or passions to trouble me, I remained the whole day shut up alone in a stove-heated room, where I had complete leisure to occupy myself with my own thoughts. One of the first of the considerations that occurred to me was that there is very often less perfection in works composed of several portions, and carried out by the hands of various masters, than in those on which one individual alone has worked. Thus we see that buildings planned and carried out by one architect alone are usually more beautiful and better proportioned than those which many have tried to put in order and improve, making use of old walls which were built with other ends in view. In the same way also, those ancient cities which, originally mere villages, have become in the process of time great towns, are usually badly constructed in comparison with those which are regularly laid out on a plain by a surveyor who is free to follow his own ideas. Even though, considering their buildings each one apart, there is often as much or more display of skill in the one case than in the other, the former have large buildings and small buildings indiscriminately placed together, thus rendering the streets crooked and irregular, so that it might be said that it was chance rather than the will of men guided by reason that led to such an arrangement. And if we consider that this happens despite the fact that from all time there have been certain officials who have had the special duty of looking after the buildings of private individuals in order that they may be public ornaments, we shall understand how difficult it is to bring about much that is satisfactory in operating only upon the works of others. Thus I imagined that those people who were once half-savage, and who have become civilized only by slow degrees, merely forming their laws as the disagreeable necessities of their crimes and quarrels constrained them, could not succeed in establishing so good a system of government as those who, from the time they first came together as communities, carried into effect the constitution laid down by some prudent legislator. Thus it is quite certain that the constitution of the true Religion whose ordinances are of God alone is incomparably better regulated than any other. And, to come down to human affairs, I believe that if Sparta was very flourishing in former times, this was not because of the excellence of each and every one of its laws, seeing that many were very strange and even contrary to good morals, but because, being drawn up by one individual, they all tended towards the same end. And similarly I thought that the sciences found in books—in those at least whose reasonings are only probable and which have no demonstrations, composed as they are of the gradually accumulated opinions of many different individuals—do not approach so near to the truth as the simple reasoning which a man of common sense can quite naturally carry out respecting the things which come immediately before him. Again I thought that since we have all been children before being men, and since it has for long fallen to us to be governed by our appetites and by our teachers (who often enough contradicted one another, and none of whom perhaps counselled us always for the best), it is almost impossible that our judgments should be so excellent or solid as they should have been had we had complete use of our reason since our birth, and had we been guided by its means alone.

It is true that we do not find that all the houses in a town are rased to the ground for the sole reason that the town is to be rebuilt in another fashion, with streets made more beautiful ; but at the same time we see that many people cause their own houses to be knocked down in order to rebuild them, and that sometimes they are forced so to do where there is danger of the houses falling of themselves, and when the foundations are not secure. From such examples I argued to myself that there was no plausibility in the claim of any private individual to reform a state by altering everything, and by overturning it throughout, in order to set it right again. Nor is it likewise probable that the whole body of the Sciences, or the order of teaching established by the Schools, should be reformed. But as regards all the opinions which up to this time I had embraced, I thought I could not do better than endeavour once for all to sweep them completely away, so that they might later on be replaced, either by others which were better, or by the same, when I had made them conform to the uniformity of a rational scheme. And I firmly believed that by this means I should succeed in directing my life much better than if I had only built on old foundations, and relied on principles of which I allowed myself to be in youth persuaded without having inquired into their truth. For although in so doing I recognised various difficulties, these were at the same time not unsurmountable, nor comparable to those which are found in reformation of the most insignificant kind in matters which concern the public. In the case of great bodies it is too difficult a task to raise them again when they are once thrown down, or even to keep them in their places when once thoroughly shaken ; and their fall cannot be otherwise than very violent. Then as to any imperfections that they may possess (and the very diversity that is found between them is sufficient to tell us that these in many cases exist) custom has doubtless greatly mitigated them, while it has also helped us to avoid, or insensibly corrected a number against which mere foresight would have found it difficult to guard. And finally the imperfections are almost always more supportable than would be the process of removing them, just as the great roads which wind about amongst the mountains become, because of being frequented, little by little so well-beaten and easy that it is much better to follow them than to try to go more directly by climbing over rocks and descending to the foot of precipices.

This is the reason why I cannot in any way approve of those turbulent and unrestful spirits who, being called neither by birth nor fortune to the management of public affairs, never fail to have always in their minds some new reforms.   And if I thought that in this treatise there was contained the smallest justification for this folly, I should be very sorry to allow it to be published.   My design has never extended beyond trying to reform my own opinion and to build on a foundation which is entirely my own.   If my work has given me a certain satisfaction, so that I here present to you a draft of it, I do not so do because I wish to advise anybody to imitate it. Those to whom God has been most beneficent in the bestowal of His graces will perhaps form designs which are more elevated; but I fear much that this particular one will seem too venturesome for many.   The simple resolve to strip oneself of all opinions and beliefs formerly received is not to be regarded as an example that each man should follow, and the world may be said to be mainly composed of two classes of minds neither of which could prudently adopt it. There are those who, believing themselves to be cleverer than they are, cannot restrain themselves from being precipitate in judgment and have not sufficient patience to arrange their thoughts in proper order; hence, once a man of this description had taken the liberty of doubting the principles he formerly accepted, and had deviated from the beaten track, he would never be able to maintain the path which must be followed to reach the appointed end more quickly, and he would hence remain wandering astray all through his life. Secondly, there are those who having reason or modesty enough to judge that they are less capable of distinguishing truth from falsehood than some others from whom instruction might be obtained, are right in contenting themselves with following the opinions of these others rather than in searching better ones for themselves.

For myself I should doubtless have been of these last if I had never had more than a single master, or had I never known the diversities which have from all time existed between the opinions of men of the greatest learning.   But I had been taught, even in my College days, that there is nothing imaginable so strange or so little credible that it has not been maintained by one philosopher or other, and I further recognised in the course of my travels that all those whose sentiments are very contrary to ours are yet not necessarily barbarians or savages, but may be possessed of reason in as great or even a greater degree than ourselves.   I also considered how very different the self-same man, identical in mind and spirit, may become, according as he is brought up from childhood amongst the French or Germans, or has passed his whole life amongst Chinese or cannibals. I likewise noticed how even in the fashions of one's clothing the same thing that pleased us ten years ago, and which will perhaps please us once again before ten years are passed, seems at the present time extravagant and ridiculous. I thus concluded that it is much more custom and example that persuade us than any certain knowledge, and yet in spite of this the voice of the majority does not afford a proof of any value in truths a little difficult to discover, because such truths are much more likely to have been discovered by one man than by a nation. I could not, however, put my finger on a single person whose opinions seemed preferable to those of others, and I found that I was, so to speak, constrained myself to undertake the direction of my procedure.

But like one who walks alone and in the twilight I resolved to go so slowly, and to use so much circumspection in all things, that if my advance was but very small, at least I guarded myself well from falling. I did not wish to set about the final rejection of any single opinion which might formerly have crept into my beliefs without having been introduced there by means of Reason, until I had first of all employed sufficient time in planning out the task which I had undertaken, and in seeking the true Method of arriving at a knowledge of all the things of which my mind was capable.

Among the different branches of Philosophy, I had in my younger days to a certain extent studied Logic; and in those of Mathematics, Geometrical Analysis and Algebra—three arts or sciences which seemed as though they ought to contribute something to the design I had in view. But in examining them I observed in respect to Logic that the syllogisms and the greater part of the other teaching served better in explaining to others those things that one knows (or like the art of Lully, in enabling one to speak without judgment of those things of which one is ignorant) than in learning what is new. And although in reality Logic contains many precepts which are very true and very good, there are at the same time mingled with them so many others which are hurtful or superfluous, that it is almost as difficult to separate the two as to draw a Diana or a Minerva out of a block of marble which is not yet roughly hewn. And as to the Analysis of the ancients and the Algebra of the moderns, besides the fact that they embrace only matters the most abstract, such as appear to have no actual use, the former is always so restricted to the consideration of symbols that it cannot exercise the Understanding without greatly fatiguing the Imagination; and in the latter one is so subjected to certain rules and formulas that the result is the construction of an art which is confused and obscure, and which embarrasses the mind, instead of a science which contributes to its cultivation. This made me feel that some other Method must be found, which, comprising the advantages of the three, is yet exempt from their faults. And as a multiplicity of laws often furnishes excuses for evil-doing, and as a State is hence much better ruled when, having but very few laws, these are most strictly observed; so, instead of the great number of precepts of which Logic is composed, I believed that I should find the four which I shall state quite sufficient, provided that I adhered to a firm and constant resolve never on any single occasion to fail in their observance.

The first of these was to accept nothing as true which I did not clearly recognise to be so : that is to say, carefully to avoid precipitation and prejudice in judgments, and to accept in them nothing more than what was presented to my mind so clearly and distinctly that I could have no occasion to doubt it.

The second was to divide up each of the difficulties which I examined into as many parts as possible, and as seemed requisite in order that it might be resolved in the best manner possible.

The third was to carry on my reflections in due order, commencing with objects that were the most simple and easy to understand, in order to rise little by little, or by degrees, to knowledge of the most complex, assuming an order, even if a fictitious one, among those which do not follow a natural sequence relatively to one another.

The last was in all cases to make enumerations so complete and reviews so general that I should be certain of having omitted nothing.

Those long chains of reasoning, simple and easy as they are, of which geometricians make use in order to arrive at the most difficult demonstrations, had caused me to imagine that all those things which fall under the cognizance of man might very likely be mutually related in the same fashion ; and that, provided only that we abstain from receiving anything as true which is not so, and always retain the order which is necessary in order to deduce the one conclusion from the other, there can be nothing so remote that we cannot reach to it, nor so recondite that we cannot discover it. And I had not much trouble in discovering which objects it was necessary to begin with, for I already knew that it was with the most simple and those most easy to apprehend. Considering also that of all those who have hitherto sought for the truth in the

Sciences, it has been the mathematicians alone who have been able to succeed in making any demonstrations, that is to say producing reasons which are evident and certain, I did not doubt that it had been by means of a similar kind that they carried on their investigations. I did not at the same time hope for any practical result in so doing, except that my mind would become accustomed to the nourishment of truth and would not content itself with false reasoning. But for all that I had no intention of trying to master all those particular sciences that receive in common the name of Mathematics; but observing that, although their objects are different, they do not fail to agree in this, that they take nothing under consideration but the various relationships or proportions which are present in these objects, I thought that it would be better if I only examined these proportions in their general aspect, and without viewing them otherwise than in the objects which would serve most to facilitate a knowledge of them. Not that I should in any way restrict them to these objects, for I might later on all the more easily apply them to all other objects to which they were applicable. Then, having carefully noted that in order to comprehend the proportions I should sometimes require to consider each one in particular, and sometimes merely keep them in mind, or take them in groups, I thought that, in order the better to consider them in detail, I should picture them in the form of lines, because I could find no method more simple nor more capable of being distinctly represented to my imagination and senses. I considered, however, that in order to keep them in my memory or to embrace several at once, it would be essential that I should explain them by means of certain formulas, the shorter the better. And for this purpose it was requisite that I should borrow all that is best in Geometrical Analysis and Algebra, and correct the errors of the one by the other.

As a matter of fact, I can venture to say that the exact observation of the few precepts which I had chosen gave me so much facility in sifting out all the questions embraced in these two sciences, that in the two or three months which I employed in examining them—commencing with the most simple and general, and making each truth that I discovered a rule for helping me to find others—not only did I arrive at the solution of many questions which I had hitherto regarded as most difficult, but, towards the end, it seemed to me that I was able to determine in the case of those of which I was still ignorant, by what means, and in how far, it was possible to

solve them.   In this I might perhaps appear to you to be very vain
if you did not remember that having but one truth to discover in
respect to each matter, whoever succeeds in finding it knows in its
regard as much as can be known.   It is the same as with a child, for
instance, who has been instructed in Arithmetic and has made an
addition according to the rule prescribed ; he may be sure of having
found as regards the sum of figures given to him all that the human
mind can know.   For, in conclusion, the Method which teaches us
to follow the true order and enumerate exactly every term in the
matter under investigation contains everything which gives certainty
to the rules of Arithmetic.

But what pleased me most in this Method was that I was certain
by its means of exercising my reason in all things, if not perfectly,
at least as well as was in my power.   And besides this, I felt in
making use of it that my mind gradually accustomed itself to conceive of its objects more accurately and distinctly ; and not having
restricted this Method to any particular matter, I promised myself to
apply it as usefully to the difficulties of other sciences as I had done to
those of Algebra.   Not that on this account I dared undertake to
examine just at once all those that might present themselves ; for
that would itself have been contrary to the order which the Method
prescribes.   But having noticed that the knowledge of these difficulties must be dependent on principles derived from Philosophy in
which I yet found nothing to be certain, I thought that it was
requisite above all to try to establish certainty in it.   I considered
also that since this endeavour is the most important in all the
world, and that in which precipitation and prejudice were most to
be feared, I should not try to grapple with it till I had attained to
a much riper age than that of three and twenty, which was the age
I had reached.   I thought, too, that I should first of all employ
much time in preparing myself for the work by eradicating from my
mind all the wrong opinions which I had up to this time accepted,
and accumulating a variety of experiences fitted later on to afford
matter for my reasonings, and by ever exercising myself in the
Method which I had prescribed, in order more and more to fortify
myself in the power of using it.

Part III.

And finally, as it is not sufficient, before commencing to rebuild the house which we inhabit, to pull it down and provide materials and an architect (or to act in this capacity ourselves, and make a careful drawing of its design), unless we have also provided ourselves with some other house where we can be comfortably lodged during the time of rebuilding, so in order that I should not remain irresolute in my actions while reason obliged me to be so in my judgments, and that I might not omit to carry on my life as happily as I could, I formed for myself a code of morals for the time being which did not consist of more than three or four maxims, which maxims I should like to enumerate to you.

The first was to obey the laws and customs of my country, adhering constantly to the religion in which by God's grace I had been instructed since my childhood, and in all other things directing my conduct by opinions the most moderate in nature, and the farthest removed from excess in all those which are commonly received and acted on by the most judicious of those with whom I might come in contact. For since I began to count my own opinions as nought, because I desired to place all under examination, I was convinced that I could not do better than follow those held by people on whose judgment reliance could be placed. And although such persons may possibly exist amongst the Persians and Chinese as well as amongst ourselves, it seemed to me that it was most expedient to bring my conduct into harmony with the ideas of those with whom I should have to live ; and that, in order to ascertain that these were their real opinions, I should observe what they did rather than what they said, not only because in the corrupt state of our manners there are few people who desire to say all that they believe, but also because many are themselves ignorant of their beliefs. For since the act of thought by which we believe a thing is different from that by which we know that we believe it, the one often exists without the other. And amongst many opinions all equally received, I chose only the most moderate, both because these are always most suited for putting into practice, and probably the best (for all excess has a tendency to be bad), and also because I should have in a less degree turned aside from the right path, supposing that I was wrong, than if, having chosen an extreme course, I found that I had chosen amiss. I also made a point of counting as excess all the engagements by means of which we limit in some degree our liberty.   Not that I hold in low esteem those laws which, in order to remedy the inconstancy of feeble souls, permit, when we have a good object in our view, that certain vows be taken, or contracts made, which oblige us to carry out that object.   This sanction is even given for security in commerce where designs are wholly indifferent.   But because I saw nothing in all the world remaining constant, and because for my own part I promised myself gradually to get my judgments to grow better and never to grow worse, I should have thought that I had committed a serious sin against commonsense if, because I approved of something at one time, I was obliged to regard it similarly at a later time, after it had possibly ceased to meet my approval, or after I had ceased to regard it in a favourable light.

My second maxim was that of being as firm and resolute in my actions as I could be, and not to follow less faithfully opinions the most dubious, when my mind was once made up regarding them, than if these had been beyond doubt.   In this I should be following the example of travellers, who, finding themselves lost in a forest, know that they ought not to wander first to one side and then to the other, nor, still less, to stop in one place, but understand that they should continue to walk as straight as they can in one direction, not diverging for any slight reason, even though it was possibly chance alone that first determined them in their choice.   By this means if they do not go exactly where they wish, they will at least arrive somewhere at the end, where probably they will be better off than in the middle of a forest.   And thus since often enough in the actions of life no delay is permissible, it is very certain that, when it is beyond our power to discern the opinions which carry most truth, we should follow the most probable ; and even although we notice no greater probability in the one opinion than in the other, we at least should make up our minds to follow a particular one and afterwards consider it as no longer doubtful in its relationship to practice, but as very true and very certain, inasmuch as the reason which caused us to determine upon it is known to be so.   And henceforward this principle was sufficient to deliver me from all the penitence and remorse which usually affect the mind and agitate the conscience of those weak and vacillating creatures who allow themselves to keep changing their procedure, and practise as good, things which they afterwards judge to be evil.

My third maxim was to try always to conquer myself rather than fortune, and to alter my desires rather than change the order of the world, and generally to accustom myself to believe that there is nothing entirely within our power but our own thoughts : so that after we have done our best in regard to the things that are without us, our ill-success cannot possibly be failure on our part[1]. And this alone seemed to me sufficient to prevent my desiring anything in the future beyond what I could actually obtain, hence rendering me content ; for since our will does not naturally induce us to desire anything but what our understanding represents to it as in some way possible of attainment, it is certain that if we consider all good things which are outside of us as equally outside of our power, we should not have more regret in resigning those goods which appear to pertain to our birth, when we are deprived of them for no fault of our own, than we have in not possessing the kingdoms of China or Mexico. In the same way, making what is called a virtue out of a necessity, we should no more desire to be well if ill, or free, if in prison, than we now do to have our bodies formed of a substance as little corruptible as diamonds, or to have wings to fly with like birds. I allow, however, that to accustom oneself to regard all things from this point of view requires long exercise and meditation often repeated ; and I believe that it is principally in this that is to be found the secret of those philosophers who, in ancient times, were able to free themselves from the empire of fortune, or, despite suffering or poverty, to rival their gods in their happiness. For, ceaselessly occupying themselves in considering the limits which were prescribed to them by nature, they persuaded themselves so completely that nothing was within their own power but their thoughts, that this conviction alone was sufficient to prevent their having any longing for other things. And they had so absolute a mastery over their thoughts that they had some reason for esteeming themselves as more rich and more powerful, and more free and more happy than other men, who, however favoured by nature or fortune they might be, if devoid of this philosophy, never could arrive at all at which they aim.

And last of all, to conclude this moral code, I felt it incumbent on me to make a review of the various occupations of men in this life in order to try to choose out the best ; and without wishing to say anything of the employment of others I thought that I could

---

[1] "So that whatever does not eventuate after we have done all in our power that it should happen is to be accounted by us as among the things which evidently cannot be done and which in philosophical phrase are called impossible." Latin Version.

not do better than continue in the one in which I found myself engaged, that is to say, in occupying my whole life in cultivating my Reason, and in advancing myself as much as possible in the knowledge of the truth in accordance with the method which I had prescribed myself. I had experienced so much satisfaction since beginning to use this method, that I did not believe that any sweeter or more innocent could in this life be found,—every day discovering by its means some truths which seemed to me sufficiently important, although commonly ignored by other men. The satisfaction which I had so filled my mind that all else· seemed of no account. And, besides, the three preceding maxims were founded solely on the plan which I had formed of continuing to instruct myself. For since God has given to each of us some light with which to distinguish truth from error, I could not believe that I ought for a single moment to content myself with accepting the opinions held by others unless I had in view the employment of my own judgment in examining them at the proper time ; and I could not have held myself free of scruple in following such opinions, if nevertheless I had not intended to lose no occasion of finding superior opinions, supposing them to exist; and finally, I should not have been able to restrain my desires nor to remain content, if I had not followed a road by which, thinking that I should be certain to be able to acquire all the knowledge of which I was capable, I also thought I should likewise be certain of obtaining all the best things which could ever come within my power. And inasmuch as our will impels us neither to follow after nor to flee from anything, excepting as our understanding represents it as good or evil, it is sufficient to judge wisely in order to act well, and the best judgment brings the best action—that is to say, the acquisition of all the virtues and all the other good things that it is possible to obtain. When one is certain that this point is reached, one cannot fail to be contented.

Having thus assured myself of these maxims, and having set them on one side along with the truths of religion which have always taken the first place in my creed, I judged that as far as the rest of my opinions were concerned, I could safely undertake to rid myself of them. And inasmuch as I hoped to be able to reach my end more successfully in converse with man than in living longer shut up in the warm room where these reflections had come to me, I hardly awaited the end of winter before I once more set myself to travel. And in all the nine following years I did nought but roam hither and thither, trying to be a spectator rather than an actor in all the comedies the world displays. More especially did I reflect in each matter that came before me as to anything which could make it subject to suspicion or doubt, and give occasion for mistake, and I rooted out of my mind all the errors which might have formerly crept in. Not that indeed I imitated the sceptics, who only doubt for the sake of doubting, and pretend to be always uncertain; for, on the contrary, my design was only to provide myself with good ground for assurance, and to reject the quicksand and mud in order to find the rock or clay. In this task it seems to me, I succeeded pretty well, since in trying to discover the error or uncertainty of the propositions which I examined, not by feeble conjectures, but by clear and assured reasonings, I encountered nothing so dubious that I could not draw from it some conclusion that was tolerably secure, if this were no more than the inference that it contained in it nothing that was certain. And just as in pulling down an old house we usually preserve the debris to serve in building up another, so in destroying all those opinions which I considered to be ill-founded, I made various observations and acquired many experiences, which have since been of use to me in establishing those which are more certain. And more than this, I continued to exercise myself in the method which I had laid down for my use; for besides the fact that I was careful as a rule to conduct all my thoughts according to its maxims, I set aside some hours from time to time which I more especially employed in practising myself in the solution of mathematical problems according to the Method, or in the solution of other problems which though pertaining to other sciences, I was able to make almost similar to those of mathematics, by detaching them from all principles of other sciences which I found to be not sufficiently secure. You will see the result in many examples which are expounded in this volume[1]. And hence, without living to all appearance in any way differently from those who, having no occupation beyond spending their lives in ease and innocence, study to separate pleasure from vice, and who, in order to enjoy their leisure without weariness, make use of all distractions that are innocent and good, I did not cease to prosecute my design, and to profit perhaps even more in my study of Truth than if I had done nothing but read books or associate with literary people.

[1] The Dioptrics, Meteors and Geometry were published originally in the same volume.

These nine years thus passed away before I had taken any definite part in regard to the difficulties as to which the learned are in the habit of disputing, or had commenced to seek the foundation of any philosophy more certain than the vulgar. And the example of many excellent men who had tried to do the same before me, but, as it appears to me, without success, made me imagine it to be so hard that possibly I should not have dared to undertake the task, had I not discovered that someone had spread abroad the report that I had already reached its conclusion. I cannot tell on what they based this opinion; if my conversation has contributed anything to it, this must have arisen from my confessing my ignorance more ingenuously than those who have studied a little usually do. And perhaps it was also due to my having shown forth my reasons for doubting many things which were held by others to be certain, rather than from having boasted of any special philosophic system. But being at heart honest enough not to desire to be esteemed as different from what I am, I thought that I must try by every means in my power to render myself worthy of the reputation which I had gained. And it is just eight years ago that this desire made me resolve to remove myself from all places where any acquaintances were possible, and to retire to a country such as this[1], where the long-continued war has caused such order to be established that the armies which are maintained seem only to be of use in allowing the inhabitants to enjoy the fruits of peace with so much the more security; and where, in the crowded throng of a great and very active nation, which is more concerned with its own affairs than curious about those of others, without missing any of the conveniences of the most populous towns, I can live as solitary and retired as in deserts the most remote.

Part IV.

I do not know that I ought to tell you of the first meditations there made by me, for they are so metaphysical and so unusual that they may perhaps not be acceptable to everyone. And yet at the same time, in order that one may judge whether the foundations which I have laid are sufficiently secure, I find myself constrained in some measure to refer to them. For a long time I had remarked that it is sometimes requisite in common life to follow opinions which one knows to be most uncertain, exactly as though they were indisputable, as has been said above. But because in this case

[1] i.e. Holland, where Descartes settled in 1629.

I wished to give myself entirely to the search after Truth, I thought that it was necessary for me to take an apparently opposite course, and to reject as absolutely false everything as to which I could imagine the least ground of doubt, in order to see if afterwards there remained anything in my belief that was entirely certain. Thus, because our senses sometimes deceive us, I wished to suppose that nothing is just as they cause us to imagine it to be; and because there are men who deceive themselves in their reasoning and fall into paralogisms, even concerning the simplest matters of geometry, and judging that I was as subject to error as was any other, I rejected as false all the reasons formerly accepted by me as demonstrations. And since all the same thoughts and conceptions which we have while awake may also come to us in sleep, without any of them being at that time true, I resolved to assume that everything that ever entered into my mind was no more true than the illusions of my dreams. But immediately afterwards I noticed that whilst I thus wished to think all things false, it was absolutely essential that the 'I' who thought this should be somewhat, and remarking that this truth '*I think, therefore I am*' was so certain and so assured that all the most extravagant suppositions brought forward by the sceptics were incapable of shaking it, I came to the conclusion that I could receive it without scruple as the first principle of the Philosophy for which I was seeking.

And then, examining attentively that which I was, I saw that I could conceive that I had no body, and that there was no world nor place where I might be; but yet that I could not for all that conceive that I was not. On the contrary, I saw from the very fact that I thought of doubting the truth of other things, it very evidently and certainly followed that I was; on the other hand if I had only ceased from thinking, even if all the rest of what I had ever imagined had really existed, I should have no reason for thinking that I had existed. From that I knew that I was a substance the whole essence or nature of which is to think, and that for its existence there is no need of any place, nor does it depend on any material thing; so that this 'me,' that is to say, the soul by which I am what I am, is entirely distinct from body, and is even more easy to know than is the latter; and even if body were not, the soul would not cease to be what it is.

After this I considered generally what in a proposition is requisite in order to be true and certain; for since I had just discovered one which I knew to be such, I thought that I ought also to know in what this certainty consisted. And having remarked that there was nothing at all in the statement ' *I think, therefore I am* ' which assures me of having thereby made a true assertion, excepting that I see very clearly that to think it is necessary to be, I came to the conclusion that I might assume, as a general rule, that the things which we conceive very clearly and distinctly are all true—remembering, however, that there is some difficulty in ascertaining which are those that we distinctly conceive.

Following upon this, and reflecting on the fact that I doubted, and that consequently my existence was not quite perfect (for I saw clearly that it was a greater perfection to know than to doubt), I resolved to inquire whence I had learnt to think of anything more perfect than I myself was ; and I recognised very clearly that this conception must proceed from some nature which was really more perfect. As to the thoughts which I had of many other things outside of me, like the heavens, the earth, light, heat, and a thousand others, I had not so much difficulty in knowing whence they came, because, remarking nothing in them which seemed to render them superior to me, I could believe that, if they were true, they were dependencies upon my nature, in so far as it possessed some perfection ; and if they were not true, that I held them from nought, that is to say, that they were in me because I had something lacking in my nature. But this could not apply to the idea of a Being more perfect than my own, for to hold it from nought would be manifestly impossible ; and because it is no less contradictory to say of the more perfect that it is what results from and depends on the less perfect, than to say that there is something which proceeds from nothing, it was equally impossible that I should hold it from myself. In this way it could but follow that it had been placed in me by a Nature which was really more perfect than mine could be, and which even had within itself all the perfections of which I could form any idea—that is to say, to put it in a word, which was God. To which I added that since I knew some perfections which I did not possess, I was not the only being in existence (I shall here use freely, if you will allow, the terms of the School) ; but that there was necessarily some other more perfect Being on which I depended, or from which I acquired all that I had. For if I had existed alone and independent of any others, so that I should have had from myself all that perfection of being in which I participated to however small an extent, I should have been able for the same reason to have had all the remainder which

I knew that I lacked; and thus I myself should have been infinite, eternal, immutable, omniscient, all-powerful, and, finally, I should have all the perfections which I could discern in God. For, in pursuance of the reasonings which I have just carried on, in order to know the nature of God as far as my nature is capable of knowing it, I had only to consider in reference to all these things of which I found some idea in myself, whether it was a perfection to possess them or not. And I was assured that none of those which indicated some imperfection were in Him, but that all else was present; and I saw that doubt, inconstancy, sadness, and such things, could not be in Him considering that I myself should have been glad to be without them. In addition to this, I had ideas of many things which are sensible and corporeal, for, although I might suppose that I was dreaming, and that all that I saw or imagined was false, I could not at the same time deny that the ideas were really in my thoughts. But because I had already recognised very clearly in myself that the nature of the intelligence is distinct from that of the body, and observing that all composition gives evidence of dependency, and that dependency is manifestly an imperfection, I came to the conclusion that it could not be a perfection in God to be composed of these two natures, and that consequently He was not so composed. I judged, however, that if there were any bodies in the world, or even any intelligences or other natures which were not wholly perfect, their existence must depend on His power in such a way that they could not subsist without Him for a single moment.

After that I desired to seek for other truths, and having put before myself the object of the geometricians, which I conceived to be a continuous body, or a space indefinitely extended in length, breadth, height or depth, which was divisible into various parts, and which might have various figures and sizes, and might be moved or transposed in all sorts of ways (for all this the geometricians suppose to be in the object of their contemplation), I went through some of their simplest demonstrations, and having noticed that this great certainty which everyone attributes to these demonstrations is founded solely on the fact that they are conceived of with clearness, in accordance with the rule which I have just laid down, I also noticed that there was nothing at all in them to assure me of the existence of their object. For, to take an example, I saw very well that if we suppose a triangle to be given, the three angles must certainly be equal to two right angles; but for all that I saw no reason to be assured that there was any such triangle in existence, while on the contrary, on reverting to the examination of the idea which I had of a Perfect Being, I found that in this case existence was implied in it in the same manner in which the equality of its three angles to two right angles is implied in the idea of a triangle; or in the idea of a sphere, that all the points on its surface are equidistant from its centre, or even more evidently still. Consequently it is at least as certain that God, who is a Being so perfect, is, or exists, as any demonstration of geometry can possibly be.

What causes many, however, to persuade themselves that there is difficulty in knowing this truth, and even in knowing the nature of their soul, is the fact that they never raise their minds above the things of sense, or that they are so accustomed to consider nothing excepting by imagining it, which is a mode of thought specially adapted to material objects, that all that is not capable of being imagined appears to them not to be intelligible at all. This is manifest enough from the fact that even the philosophers in the Schools hold it as a maxim that there is nothing in the understanding which has not first of all been in the senses, in which there is certainly no doubt that the ideas of God and of the soul have never been. And it seems to me that those who desire to make use of their imagination in order to understand these ideas, act in the same way as if, to hear sounds or smell odours, they should wish to make use of their eyes : excepting that there is indeed this difference, that the sense of sight does not give us less assurance of the truth of its objects, than do those of scent or of hearing, while neither our imagination nor our senses can ever assure us of anything, if our understanding does not intervene.

If there are finally any persons who are not sufficiently persuaded of the existence of God and of their soul by the reasons which I have brought forward, I wish that they should know that all other things of which they perhaps think themselves more assured (such as possessing a body, and that there are stars and an earth and so on) are less certain. For, although we have a moral assurance of these things which is such that it seems that it would be extravagant in us to doubt them, at the same time no one, unless he is devoid of reason, can deny, when a metaphysical certainty is in question, that there is sufficient cause for our not having complete assurance, by observing the fact that when asleep we may similarly imagine that we have another body, and that we see other stars and another earth, without there being anything of the kind.

For how do we know that the thoughts that come in dreams are
more false than those that we have when we are awake, seeing that
often enough the former are not less lively and vivid than the
latter? And though the wisest minds may study the matter as
much as they will, I do not believe that they will be able to give
any sufficient reason for removing this doubt, unless they presuppose
the existence of God. For to begin with, that which I have just
taken as a rule, that is to say, that all the things that we very
clearly and very distinctly conceive of are true, is certain only
because God is or exists, and that He is a Perfect Being, and that
all that is in us issues from Him. From this it follows that our
ideas or notions, which to the extent of their being clear or distinct
are ideas of real things issuing from God, cannot but to that extent
be true. So that though we often enough have ideas which have
an element of falsity, this can only be the case in regard to those
which have in them somewhat that is confused or obscure, because
in so far as they have this character they participate in negation
—that is, they exist in us as confused only because we are not
quite perfect. And it is evident that there is no less repugnance
in the idea that error or imperfection, inasmuch as it is imperfection, proceeds from God, than there is in the idea of truth or
perfection proceeding from nought. But if we did not know that
all that is in us of reality and truth proceeds from a perfect and
infinite Being, however clear and distinct were our ideas, we should
not have any reason to assure ourselves that they had the perfection
of being true.

But after the knowledge of God and of the soul has thus
rendered us certain of this rule, it is very easy to understand that
the dreams which we imagine in our sleep should not make us in
any way doubt the truth of the thoughts which we have when
awake. For even if in sleep we had some very distinct idea such as
a geometrician might have who discovered some new demonstration,
the fact of being asleep would not militate against its truth. And
as to the most ordinary error in our dreams, which consists in
their representing to us various objects in the same way as do our
external senses, it does not matter that this should give us occasion
to suspect the truth of such ideas, because we may be likewise often
enough deceived in them without our sleeping at all, just as when
those who have the jaundice see everything as yellow, or when stars
or other bodies which are very remote appear much smaller than
they really are. For, finally, whether we are awake or asleep, we

should never allow ourselves to be persuaded excepting by the evidence of our Reason. And it must be remarked that I speak of our Reason and not of our imagination nor of our senses; just as though we see the sun very clearly, we should not for that reason judge that it is of the size of which it appears to be; likewise we could quite well distinctly imagine the head of a lion on the body of a goat, without necessarily concluding that a chimera exists. For Reason does not insist that whatever we see or imagine thus is a truth, but it tells us clearly that all our ideas or notions must have some foundation of truth. For otherwise it could not be possible that God, who is all perfection and truth, should have placed them within us. And because our reasonings are never so evident nor so complete during sleep as during wakefulness, although sometimes our imaginations are then just as lively and acute, or even more so, Reason tells us that since our thoughts cannot possibly be all true, because we are not altogether perfect, that which they have of truth must infallibly be met with in our waking experience rather than in that of our dreams.

PART V.

I should be very glad to proceed to show forth the complete chain of truths which I have deduced from these first, but because to do this it would have been necessary now to speak of many matters of dispute among the learned, with whom I have no desire to embroil myself, I think that it will be better to abstain. I shall only state generally what these truths are, so that it may be left to the decision of those best able to judge whether it would be of use for the public to be more particularly informed of them or not. I always remained firm in the resolution which I had made, not to assume any other principle than that of which I have just made use, in order to demonstrate the existence of God and of the Soul, and to accept nothing as true which did not appear to be more clear and more certain than the demonstrations of the geometricians had formerly seemed. And nevertheless I venture to say that not only have I found the means of satisfying myself in a short time as to the more important of those difficulties usually dealt with in philosophy, but I have also observed certain laws which God has so established in Nature, and of which He has imprinted such ideas on our minds, that, after having reflected sufficiently upon the matter, we cannot doubt their being accurately observed in all that exists or is done in the world. Further, in considering the sequence of these laws, it seems to me that I have discovered many truths more useful and more important than all that I had formerly learned or even hoped to learn.

But because I tried to explain the most important of these in a Treatise[1] which certain considerations prevented me from publishing, I cannot do better, in making them known, than here summarise briefly what that Treatise contains. I had planned to comprise in it all that I believed myself to know regarding the nature of material objects, before I set myself to write. However, just as the painters who cannot represent equally well on a plain surface all the various sides of a solid body, make selection of one of the most important, which alone is set in the light, while the others are put in shadow and made to appear only as they may be seen in looking at the former, so, fearing that I could not put in my Treatise all that I had in my mind, I undertook only to show very fully my conceptions of light. Later on, when occasion occurred, I resolved to add something about the sun and fixed stars, because light proceeds almost entirely from them ; the heavens would be dealt with because they transmit light, the planets, the comets and the earth because they reflect it, and more particularly would all bodies which are on the earth, because they are either coloured or transparent, or else luminous ; and finally I should deal with man because he is the spectator of all. For the very purpose of putting all these topics somewhat in shadow, and being able to express myself freely about them, without being obliged to adopt or to refute the opinions which are accepted by the learned, I resolved to leave all this world to their disputes, and to speak only of what would happen in a new world if God now created, somewhere in an imaginary space, matter sufficient where-with to form it, and if He agitated in diverse ways, and without any order, the diverse portions of this matter, so that there resulted a chaos as confused as the poets ever feigned, and concluded His work by merely lending His concurrence to Nature in the usual way, leaving her to act in accordance with the laws which He had established. So, to begin with, I described this matter and tried to represent it in such a way, that it seems to me that nothing in the world could be more clear or intelligible, excepting what has just been said of God and the Soul. For I even went so far as expressly to assume that there was in it none of these forms or qualities which are so debated in the Schools, nor anything at all the

---

[1] i.e. ‘Le Monde,’ suppressed on hearing of Galileo’s condemnation.

knowledge of which is not so natural to our minds that none could even pretend to be ignorant of it. Further I pointed out what are the laws of Nature, and, without resting my reasons on any other principle than the infinite perfections of God, I tried to demonstrate all those of which one could have any doubt, and to show that they are of such a nature that even if God had created other worlds, He could not have created any in which these laws would fail to be observed. After that, I showed how the greatest part of the matter of which this chaos is constituted, must, in accordance with these laws, dispose and arrange itself in such a fashion as to render it similar to our heavens; and how meantime some of its parts must form an earth, some planets and comets, and some others a sun and fixed stars. And, enlarging on the subject of light, I here explained at length the nature of the light which would be found in the sun and stars, and how from these it crossed in an instant the immense space of the heavens, and how it was reflected from the planets and comets to the earth. To this I also added many things touching the substance, situation, movements, and all the different qualities of these heavens and stars, so that I thought I had said enough to make it clear that there is nothing to be seen in the heavens and stars pertaining to our system which must not, or at least may not, appear exactly the same in those of the system which I described. From this point I came to speak more particularly of the earth, showing how, though I had expressly presupposed that God had not placed any weight in the matter of which it is composed, its parts did not fail all to gravitate exactly to its centre; and how, having water and air on its surface, the disposition of the heavens and of the stars, more particularly of the moon, must cause a flux or reflux, which in all its circumstances is similar to that which is observed in our seas, and besides that, a certain current both of water and air from east to west, such as may also be observed in the tropics. I also showed how the mountains, seas, fountains and rivers, could naturally be formed in it, how the metals came to be in the mines and the plants to grow in the fields; and generally how all bodies, called mixed or composite, might arise. And because I knew nothing but fire which could produce light, excepting the stars, I studied amongst other things to make very clear all that pertains to its nature, how it is formed, how nourished, how there is sometimes only heat without light, and sometimes light without heat; I showed, too, how different colours might by it be induced upon different bodies and qualities of diverse kinds, how

some of these were liquefied and others solidified, how nearly all can
be consumed or converted into ashes and smoke by its means, and
finally how of these ashes, by the intensity of its action alone, it
forms glass.   Since this transformation of ashes into glass seemed
to me as wonderful as any other process in nature, I took particular
pleasure in describing it.

I did not at the same time wish to infer from all these facts
that this world has been created in the manner which I described ;
for it is much more probable that at the beginning God made it
such as it was to be.   But it is certain, and it is an opinion
commonly received by the theologians, that the action by which
He now preserves it is just the same as that by which He at first
created it.   In this way, although He had not, to begin with, given
this world any other form than that of chaos, provided that the
laws of nature had once been established and that He had lent His
aid in order that its action should be according to its wont, we may
well believe, without doing outrage to the miracle of creation, that
by this means alone all things which are purely material might in
course of time have become such as we observe them to be at
present ; and their nature is much easier to understand when we
see them coming to pass little by little in this manner, than were
we to consider them as all complete to begin with.

From a description of inanimate bodies and plants I passed on
to that of animals, and particularly to that of men.   But since
I had not yet sufficient knowledge to speak of them in the same
style as of the rest, that is to say, demonstrating the effects from
the causes, and showing from what beginnings and in what fashion
Nature must produce them, I contented myself with supposing that
God formed the body of man altogether like one of ours, in the
outward figure of its members as well as in the interior conformation
of its organs, without making use of any matter other than that
which I had described, and without at the first placing in it a
rational soul, or any other thing which might serve as a vegetative
or as a sensitive soul; excepting that He kindled in the heart one of
these fires without light, which I have already described, and which
I did not conceive of as in any way different from that which makes
the hay heat when shut up before it is dry, and which makes new
wine grow frothy when it is left to ferment over the fruit.   For,
examining the functions which might in accordance with this supposition exist in this body, I found precisely all those which might
exist in us without our having the power of thought, and con-

sequently without our soul—that is to say, this part of us, distinct
from the body, of which it has just been said that its nature is to
think—contributing to it, functions which are identically the same
as those in which animals lacking reason may be said to resemble
us.   For all that, I could not find in these functions any which,
being dependent on thought, pertain to us alone, inasmuch as we
are men; while I found all of them afterwards, when I assumed
that God had created a rational soul and that He had united it
to this body in a particular manner which I described.

But in order to show how I there treated of this matter, I wish here
to set forth the explanation of the movement of heart and arteries
which, being the first and most general movement that is observed
in animals, will give us the means of easily judging as to what we
ought to think about all the rest.   And so that there may be less
difficulty in understanding what I shall say on this matter, I should
like that those not versed in anatomy should take the trouble, before
reading this, of having cut up before their eyes the heart of some
large animal which has lungs (for it is in all respects sufficiently
similar to the heart of a man), and cause that there be demonstrated
to them the two chambers or cavities which are within it.   There is
first of all that which is on the right side, with which two very large
tubes or channels correspond, viz. the *vena cava*, which is the
principal receptacle of the blood, and so to speak the trunk of a
tree of which all the other veins of the body are the branches ; and
there is the arterial vein which has been badly named because it
is nothing but an artery which, taking its origin from the heart,
divides, after having issued from it, into many branches which
proceed to disperse themselves all through the lungs.   Then there
is secondly the cavity on the left side with which there again
correspond two tubes which are as large or larger than the preceding, viz. the venous artery, which has also been badly named,
because it is nothing but a vein which comes from the lungs, where
it is divided into many branches, interlaced with those of the
arterial vein, and with those of the tube which is called the windpipe,
through which enters the air which we breathe ; and the great
artery which, issuing from the heart, sends its branches throughout
the body.   I should also wish that the eleven little membranes,
which, like so many doors, open and shut the four entrances which
are in these two cavities, should be carefully shown.   There are of
these three at the entrance of the *vena cava*, where they are so
arranged that they can in nowise prevent the blood which it contains

from flowing into the right cavity of the heart and yet exactly prevent its issuing out ; there are three at the entrance to the arterial vein, which, being arranged quite the other way, easily allow the blood which is in this cavity to pass into the lungs, but not that which is already in the lungs to return to this cavity. There are also two others at the entrance of the venous artery, which allow the blood in the lungs to flow towards the left cavity of the heart, but do not permit its return ; and three at the entrance of the great artery, which allow the blood to flow from the heart, but prevent its return. There is then no cause to seek for any other reason for the number of these membranes, except that the opening of the venous artery being oval, because of the situation where it is met with, may be conveniently closed with two membranes, while the others, being round, can be better closed with three. Further, I should have my readers consider that the grand artery and the arterial vein are much harder and firmer than are the venous artery and the *vena cava* ; and that these two last expand before entering the heart, and there form so to speak two pockets called the auricles of the heart, which are composed of a tissue similar to its own ; and also that there is always more heat in the heart than in any other part of the body ; and finally that this heat is capable of causing any drop of blood that enters into its cavities promptly to expand and dilate, as liquids usually do when they are allowed to fall drop by drop into some very hot vessel.

After this I do not need to say anything with a view to explaining the movement of the heart, except that when its cavities are not full of blood there necessarily flows from the *vena cava* into the right cavity, and from the venous artery into the left, enough blood to keep these two vessels always full, and being full, that their orifices, which are turned towards the heart, cannot then be closed. But as soon as two drops of blood have thus entered, one into each of the cavities, these drops, which cannot be otherwise than very large, because the openings by which they enter are very wide and the vessels from whence they come are very full of blood, rarefy and dilate because of the heat which they find there. By this means, causing the whole heart to expand, they force home and close the five little doors which are at the entrances of the two vessels whence they flow, thus preventing any more blood from coming down into the heart ; and becoming more and more rarefied, they push open the six doors which are in the entrances of the two other vessels through which they make their exit, by this means causing

all the branches of the arterial vein and of the great artery to expand
almost at the same instant as the heart. This last immediately
afterward contracts as do also the arteries, because the blood which
has entered them has cooled ; and the six little doors close up again,
and the five doors of the *vena cava* and of the venous artery re-open
and make a way for two other drops of blood which cause the heart
and the arteries once more to expand, just as we saw before.   And
because the blood which then enters the heart passes through these
two pouches which are called auricles, it comes to pass that their
movement is contrary to the movement of the heart, and that they
contract when it expands.   For the rest, in order that those who
do not know the force of mathematical demonstration and are
unaccustomed to distinguish true reasons from merely probable
reasons, should not venture to deny what has been said without
examination, I wish to acquaint them with the fact that this
movement which I have just explained follows as necessarily from
the very disposition of the organs, as can be seen by looking at the
heart, and from the heat which can be felt with the fingers, and
from the nature of the blood of which we can learn by experience,
as does that of a clock from the power, the situation, and the form,
of its counterpoise and of its wheels.

But if we ask how the blood in the veins does not exhaust itself
in thus flowing continually into the heart, and how the arteries do
not become too full of blood, since all that passes through the heart
flows into them, I need only reply by stating what has already been
written by an English physician[1], to whom the credit of having
broken the ice in this matter must be ascribed, as also of being the
first to teach that there are many little tubes at the extremities of
the arteries whereby the blood that they receive from the heart
enters the little branches of the veins, whence it returns once
more to the heart; in this way its course is just a perpetual
circulation.   He proves this very clearly by the common experience
of surgeons, who, by binding the arm moderately firmly above the
place where they open the vein, cause the blood to issue more
abundantly than it would have done if they had not bound it at
all ; while quite a contrary result would occur if they bound it
below, between the hand and the opening, or if they bound it very
firmly above.   For it is clear that when the bandage is moderately
tight, though it may prevent the blood already in the arm from

[1] Harvey (Latin Tr.).

returning to the heart by the veins, it cannot for all that prevent more blood from coming anew by the arteries, because these are situated below the veins, and their walls, being stronger, are less easy to compress; and also that the blood which comes from the heart tends to pass by means of the arteries to the hand with greater force than it does to return from the hand to the heart by the veins. And because this blood escapes from the arm by the opening which is made in one of the veins, there must necessarily be some passages below the ligature, that is to say, towards the extremities of the arm, through which it can come thither from the arteries. This physician likewise proves very clearly the truth of that which he says of the course of the blood, by the existence of certain little membranes or valves which are so arranged in different places along the course of the veins, that they do not permit the blood to pass from the middle of the body towards the extremities, but only to return from the extremities to the heart; and further by the experiment which shows that all the blood which is in the body may issue from it in a very short time by means of one single artery that has been cut, and this is so even when it is very tightly bound very near the heart, and cut between it and the ligature, so that there could be no ground for supposing that the blood which flowed out of it could proceed from any other place but the heart.

But there are many other things which demonstrate that the true cause of this motion of the blood is that which I have stated. To begin with, the difference which is seen between the blood which issues from the veins, and that which issues from the arteries, can only proceed from the fact, that, being rarefied, and so to speak distilled by passing through the heart, it is more subtle and lively and warmer immediately after leaving the heart (that is to say, when in the arteries) than it is a little while before entering it (that is, when in the veins). And if attention be paid, we shall find that this difference does not appear clearly, excepting in the vicinity of the heart, and is not so clear in those parts which are further removed from it. Further, the consistency of the coverings of which the arterial vein and the great artery are composed, shows clearly enough that the blood beats against them with more force than it does in the case of the veins. And why should the left cavity of the heart and the great artery be larger and wider than the right cavity and the arterial vein, if it is not that the blood of the venous artery having only been in the lungs since it had passed through the heart, is more subtle and rarefies more effectively and

easily than that which proceeds immediately from the *vena cava*?
And what is it that the physicians can discover in feeling the pulse,
unless they know that, according as the blood changes its nature, it
may be rarefied by the warmth of the heart in a greater or less
degree, and more or less quickly than before? And if we inquire
how this heat is communicated to the other members, must it not
be allowed that it is by means of the blood which, passing through
the heart, is heated once again and thence is spread throughout
all the body? From this it happens that if we take away the blood
from any particular part, by that same means we take away from it
the heat; even if the heart were as ardent as a red hot iron it
would not suffice to heat up the feet and hands as it actually does,
unless it continually sent out to them new blood. We further
understand from this that the true use of respiration is to carry
sufficient fresh air into the lungs to cause the blood, which comes
there from the right cavity of the heart, where it has been rarefied
and so to speak transformed into vapours, to thicken, and become
anew converted into blood before falling into the left cavity, without
which process it would not be fit to serve as fuel for the fire which
there exists. We are confirmed in this statement by seeing that
the animals which have no lungs have also but one cavity in their
hearts, and that in children, who cannot use them while still within
their mother's wombs, there is an opening by which the blood flows
from the *vena cava* into the left cavity of the heart, and a conduit
through which it passes from the arterial vein into the great artery
without passing through the lung. Again, how could digestion be
carried on in the stomach if the heart did not send heat there by
the arteries, and along with this some of the more fluid parts of
the blood which aid in dissolving the foods which have been there
placed? And is not the action which converts the juice of foods
into blood easy to understand if we consider that it is distilled by
passing and repassing through the heart possibly more than one or
two hundred times in a day? What further need is there to explain
the process of nutrition and the production of the different humours
which are in the body, if we can say that the force with which
the blood, in being rarefied, passes from the heart towards the
extremities of the arteries, causes some of its parts to remain among
those of the members where they are found and there to take the
place of others which they oust; and that according to the situation
or form or smallness of the little pores which they encounter,
certain ones proceed to certain parts rather than others, just as

a number of different sieves variously perforated, as everyone has probably seen, are capable of separating different species of grain? And finally what in all this is most remarkable of all, is the generation of the animal spirits, which resemble a very subtle wind, or rather a flame which is very pure and very vivid, and which, continually rising up in great abundance from the heart to the brain, thence proceeds through the nerves to the muscles, thereby giving the power of motion to all the members. And it is not necessary to suppose any other cause to explain how the particles of blood, which, being most agitated and most penetrating, are the most proper to constitute these spirits, proceed towards the brain rather than elsewhere, than that the arteries which carry them thither are those which proceed from the heart in the most direct lines, and that according to the laws of Mechanics, which are identical with those of Nature, when many objects tend to move together to the same point, where there is not room for all (as is the case with the particles of blood which issue from the left cavity of the heart and tend to go towards the brain), the weakest and least agitated parts must necessarily be turned aside by those that are stronger, which by this means are the only ones to reach it.

I had explained all these matters in some detail in the Treatise which I formerly intended to publish. And afterwards I had shown there, what must be the fabric of the nerves and muscles of the human body in order that the animal spirits therein contained should have the power to move the members, just as the heads of animals, a little while after decapitation, are still observed to move and bite the earth, notwithstanding that they are no longer animate; what changes are necessary in the brain to cause wakefulness, sleep and dreams; how light, sounds, smells, tastes, heat and all other qualities pertaining to external objects are able to imprint on it various ideas by the intervention of the senses; how hunger, thirst and other internal affections can also convey their impressions upon it; what should be regarded as the 'common sense' by which these ideas are received, and what is meant by the memory which retains them, by the fancy which can change them in diverse ways and out of them constitute new ideas, and which, by the same means, distributing the animal spirits through the muscles, can cause the members of such a body to move in as many diverse ways, and in a manner as suitable to the objects which present themselves to its senses and to its internal passions, as can happen in our own case apart from the direction of our free will. And this will not seem strange to those, who, knowing how many different *automata* or moving machines can be made by the industry of man, without employing in so doing more than a very few parts in comparison with the great multitude of bones, muscles, nerves, arteries, veins, or other parts that are found in the body of each animal.   From this aspect the body is regarded as a machine which, having been made by the hands of God, is incomparably better arranged, and possesses in itself movements which are much more admirable, than any of those which can be invented by man.   Here I specially stopped to show that if there had been such machines, possessing the organs and outward form of a monkey or some other animal without reason, we should not have had any means of ascertaining that they were not of the same nature as those animals.   On the other hand, if there were machines which bore a resemblance to our body and imitated our actions as far as it was morally possible to do so, we should always have two very certain tests by which to recognise that, for all that, they were not real men.   The first is, that they could never use speech or other signs as we do when placing our thoughts on record for the benefit of others.   For we can easily understand a machine's being constituted so that it can utter words, and even emit some responses to action on it of a corporeal kind, which brings about a change in its organs ; for instance, if it is touched in a particular part it may ask what we wish to say to it ; if in another part it may exclaim that it is being hurt, and so on. But it never happens that it arranges its speech in various ways, in order to reply appropriately to everything that may be said in its presence, as even the lowest type of man can do.   And the second difference is, that although machines can perform certain things as well as or perhaps better than any of us can do, they infallibly fall short in others, by the which means we may discover that they did not act from knowledge, but only from the disposition of their organs.   For while reason is a universal instrument which can serve for all contingencies, these organs have need of some special adaptation for every particular action.   From this it follows that it is morally impossible that there should be sufficient diversity in any machine to allow it to act in all the events of life in the same way as our reason causes us to act.

By these two methods we may also recognise the difference that exists between men and brutes.   For it is a very remarkable fact that there are none so depraved and stupid, without even excepting idiots, that they cannot arrange different words together, forming of them a statement by which they make known their thoughts; while, on the other hand, there is no other animal, however perfect and fortunately circumstanced it may be, which can do the same. It is not the want of organs that brings this to pass, for it is evident that magpies and parrots are able to utter words just like ourselves, and yet they cannot speak as we do, that is, so as to give evidence that they think of what they say. On the other hand, men who, being born deaf and dumb, are in the same degree, or even more than the brutes, destitute of the organs which serve the others for talking, are in the habit of themselves inventing certain signs by which they make themselves understood by those who, being usually in their company, have leisure to learn their language. And this does not merely show that the brutes have less reason than men, but that they have none at all, since it is clear that very little is required in order to be able to talk. And when we notice the inequality that exists between animals of the same species, as well as between men, and observe that some are more capable of receiving instruction than others, it is not credible that a monkey or a parrot, selected as the most perfect of its species, should not in these matters equal the stupidest child to be found, or at least a child whose mind is clouded, unless in the case of the brute the soul were of an entirely different nature from ours. And we ought not to confound speech with natural movements which betray passions and may be imitated by machines as well as be manifested by animals; nor must we think, as did some of the ancients, that brutes talk, although we do not understand their language. For if this were true, since they have many organs which are allied to our own, they could communicate their thoughts to us just as easily as to those of their own race. It is also a very remarkable fact that although there are many animals which exhibit more dexterity than we do in some of their actions, we at the same time observe that they do not manifest any dexterity at all in many others. Hence the fact that they do better than we do, does not prove that they are endowed with mind, for in this case they would have more reason than any of us, and would surpass us in all other things. It rather shows that they have no reason at all, and that it is nature which acts in them according to the disposition of their organs, just as a clock, which is only composed of wheels and weights is able to tell the hours and measure the time more correctly than we can do with all our wisdom.

I had described after this the rational soul and shown that it could not be in any way derived from the power of matter, like the other things of which I had spoken, but that it must be expressly created. I showed, too, that it is not sufficier ; that it should be lodged in the human body like a pilot in his ship, unless perhaps for the moving of its members, but that it is necessary that it should also be joined and united more closely to the body in order to have sensations and appetites similar to our own, and thus to form a true man. In conclusion, I have here enlarged a little on the subject of the soul, because it is one of the greatest importance. For next to the error of those who deny God, which I think I have already sufficiently refuted, there is none which is more effectual in leading feeble spirits from the straight path of virtue, than to imagine that the soul of the brute is of the same nature as our own, and that in consequence, after this life we have nothing to fear or to hope for, any more than the flies and ants. As a matter of fact, when one comes to know how greatly they differ, we understand much better the reasons which go to prove that our soul is in its nature entirely independent of body, and in consequence that it is not liable to die with it. And then, inasmuch as we observe no other causes capable of destroying it, we are naturally inclined to judge that it is immortal.

Part VI.

It is three years since I arrived at the end of the Treatise which contained all these things; and I was commencing to revise it in order to place it in the hands of a printer, when I learned that certain persons, to whose opinions I defer, and whose authority cannot have less weight with my actions than my own reason has over my thoughts, had disapproved of a physical theory published a little while before by another person[1]. I will not say that I agreed with this opinion, but only that before their censure I observed in it nothing which I could possibly imagine to be prejudicial either to Religion or the State, or consequently which could have prevented me from giving expression to it in writing, if my reason had persuaded me to do so : and this made me fear that among my own opinions one might be found which should be misunderstood, notwithstanding the great care which I have always taken not to accept any new beliefs unless I had very certain proof of their truth, and not to give expression to what could tend to the dis-

[1] i.e. Galileo.

advantage of any person. This sufficed to cause me to alter the resolution which I had made to publish. For, although the reasons for my former resolution were very strong, my inclination, which always made me hate the profession of writing books, caused me immediately to find plenty of other reasons for excusing myself from doing so. And these reasons, on the one side and on the other, are of such a nature that not only have I here some interest in giving expression to them, but possibly the public may also have some interest in knowing them.

I have never made much of those things which proceed from my own mind, and so long as I culled no other fruits from the Method which I use, beyond that of satisfying myself respecting certain difficulties which pertain to the speculative sciences, or trying to regulate my conduct by the reasons which it has taught me, I never believed myself to be obliged to write anything about it. For as regards that which concerns conduct, everyone is so confident of his own common sense, that there might be found as many reformers as heads, if it were permitted that others than those whom God has established as the sovereigns of his people, or at least to whom He has given sufficient grace and zeal to be prophets, should be allowed to make any changes in that. And, although my speculations give me the greatest pleasure, I believed that others also had speculations which possibly pleased them even more. But so soon as I had acquired some general notions concerning Physics, and as, beginning to make use of them in various special difficulties, I observed to what point they might lead us, and how much they differ from the principles of which we have made use up to the present time, I believed that I could not keep them concealed without greatly sinning against the law which obliges us to procure, as much as in us lies, the general good of all mankind. For they caused me to see that it is possible to attain knowledge which is very useful in life, and that, instead of that speculative philosophy which is taught in the Schools, we may find a practical philosophy by means of which, knowing the force and the action of fire, water, air, the stars, heavens and all other bodies that environ us, as distinctly as we know the different crafts of our artisans, we can in the same way employ them in all those uses to which they are adapted, and thus render ourselves the masters and possessors of nature. This is not merely to be desired with a view to the invention of an infinity of arts and crafts which enable us to enjoy without any trouble the fruits of the earth and all the good things which are to be found there, but also principally because it brings about the preservation of health, which is without doubt the chief blessing and the foundation of all other blessings in this life.   For the mind depends so much on the temperament and disposition of the bodily organs that, if it is possible to find a means of rendering men wiser and cleverer than they have hitherto been, I believe that it is in medicine that it must be sought.   It is true that the medicine which is now in vogue contains little of which the utility is remarkable; but, without having any intention of decrying it, I am sure that there is no one, even among those who make its study a profession, who does not confess that all that men know is almost nothing in comparison with what remains to be known; and that we could be free of an infinitude of maladies both of body and mind, and even also possibly of the infirmities of age, if we had sufficient knowledge of their causes, and of all the remedies with which nature has provided us.   But, having the intention of devoting all my life to the investigation of a knowledge which is so essential, and having discovered a path which appears to me to be of such a nature that we must by its means infallibly reach our end if we pursue it, unless, indeed, we are prevented by the shortness of life or by lack of experience, I judged that there was no better provision against these two impediments than faithfully to communicate to the public the little which I should myself have discovered, and to beg all well-inclined persons to proceed further by contributing, each one according to his own inclination and ability, to the experiments which must be made, and then to communicate to the public all the things which they might discover, in order that the last should commence where the preceding had left off; and thus, by joining together the lives and labours of many, we should collectively proceed much further than any one in particular could succeed in doing.

I remarked also respecting experiments, that they become so much the more necessary the more one is advanced in knowledge, for to begin with it is better to make use simply of those which present themselves spontaneously to our senses, and of which we could not be ignorant provided that we reflected ever so little, rather than to seek out those which are more rare and recondite; the reason of this is that those which are more rare often mislead us so long as we do not know the causes of the more common, and the fact that the circumstances on which they depend are almost always so particular and so minute that it is very difficult to observe

them.   But in this the order which I have followed is as follows :
I have first tried to discover generally the principles or first causes
of everything that is or that can be in the world, without considering anything that might accomplish this end but God Himself who
has created the world, or deriving them from any source excepting
from certain germs of truths which are naturally existent in our
souls.   After that I considered which were the primary and most
ordinary effects which might be deduced from these causes, and it
seems to me that in this way I discovered the heavens, the stars,
an earth, and even on the earth, water, air, fire, the minerals and
some other such things, which are the most common and simple of
any that exist, and consequently the easiest to know.   Then, when
I wished to descend to those which were more particular, so many
objects of various kinds presented themselves to me, that I did not
think it was possible for the human mind to distinguish the forms or
species of bodies which are on the earth from an infinitude of others
which might have been so if it had been the will of God to place
them there, or consequently to apply them to our use, if it were not
that we arrive at the causes by the effects, and avail ourselves of
many particular experiments.   In subsequently passing over in my
mind all the objects which have ever been presented to my senses,
I can truly venture to say that I have not there observed anything
which I could not easily explain by the principles which I had
discovered.   But I must also confess that the power of nature is so
ample and so vast, and these principles are so simple and general,
that I observed hardly any particular effect as to which I could not
at once recognise that it might be deduced from the principles in
many different ways; and my greatest difficulty is usually to discover
in which of these ways the effect does depend upon them.   As to
that, I do not know any other plan but again to try to find experiments of such a nature that their result is not the same if it has to
be explained by one of the methods, as it would be if explained by
the other.   For the rest, I have now reached a position in which
I discern, as it seems to me, sufficiently clearly what course must
be adopted in order to make the majority of the experiments which
may conduce to carry out this end.   But I also perceive that they
are of such a nature, and of so great a number, that neither my
hands nor my income, though the latter were a thousand times larger
than it is, could suffice for the whole ; so that just in proportion as
henceforth I shall have the power of carrying out more of them or
less, shall I make more or less progress in arriving at a knowledge

of nature.   This is what I had promised myself to make known by
the Treatise which I had written, and to demonstrate in it so clearly
the advantage which the public might receive from it, that I should
induce all those who have the good of mankind at heart—that is to
say, all those who are really virtuous in fact, and not only by a false
semblance or by opinion—both to communicate to me those experiments that they have already carried out, and to help me in the
investigation of those that still remain to be accomplished.

But I have since that time found other reasons which caused me
to change my opinion, and consider that I should indeed continue
to put in writing all the things which I judged to be of importance
whenever I discovered them to be true, and that I should bestow on
them the same care as I should have done had I wished to have
them printed.   I did this because it would give me so much the
more occasion to examine them carefully (for there is no doubt that
we always scrutinize more closely what we think will be seen by
many, than what is done simply for ourselves, and often the things
which have seemed true to me when I began to think about them,
seemed false when I tried to place them on paper); and because
I did not desire to lose any opportunity of benefiting the public if
I were able to do so, and in order that if my works have any value,
those into whose hands they will fall after my death, might have the
power of making use of them as seems best to them.   I, however,
resolved that I should not consent to their being published during
my lifetime, so that neither the contradictions and controversies to
which they might possibly give rise, nor even the reputation, such
as it might be, which they would bring to me, should give me any
occasion to lose the time which I meant to set apart for my own
instruction.   For although it is true that each man is obliged to
procure, as much as in him lies, the good of others, and that to be
useful to nobody is popularly speaking to be worthless, it is at the
same time true that our cares should extend further than the
present time, and that it is good to set aside those things which
may possibly be adapted to bring profit to the living, when we have
in view the accomplishment of other ends which will bring much
more advantage to our descendants.   In the same way I should
much like that men should know that the little which I have
learned hitherto is almost nothing in comparison with that of which
I am ignorant, and with the knowledge of which I do not despair of
being able to attain.   For it is much the same with those who little
by little discover the truth in the Sciences, as with those who,

commencing to become rich, have less trouble in obtaining great acquisitions than they formerly experienced, when poorer, in arriving at those much smaller in amount. Or we might compare them to the Generals of our armies, whose forces usually grow in proportion to their victories, and who require more leadership in order to hold together their troops after the loss of a battle, than is needed to take towns and provinces after having obtained a success. For he really gives battle who attempts to conquer all the difficulties and errors which prevent him from arriving at a knowledge of the truth, and it is to lose a battle to admit a false opinion touching a matter of any generality and importance. Much more skill is required in order to recover the position that one beforehand held, than is necessary to make great progress when one already possesses principles which are assured. For myself, if I have succeeded in discovering certain truths in the Sciences (and I hope that the matters contained in this volume will show that I have discovered some), I may say that they are resultant from, and dependent on, five or six principal difficulties which I have surmounted, and my encounter with these I look upon as so many battles in which I have had fortune on my side. I will not even hesitate to say that I think I shall have no need to win more than two or three other victories similar in kind in order to reach the accomplishment of my plans. And my age is not so advanced but that, in the ordinary course of nature, I may still have sufficient leisure for this end. But I believe myself to be so much the more bound to make the most of the time which remains, as I have the greater hope of being able to employ it well. And without doubt I should have many chances of being robbed of it, were I to publish the foundations of my Physics ; for though these are nearly all so evident that it is only necessary to understand them in order to accept them, and although there are none of them as to which I do not believe myself capable of giving demonstration, yet because it is impossible that they should accord with all the various opinions of other men, I foresee that I should often be diverted from my main design by the opposition which they would bring to birth.

We may say that these contradictions might be useful both in making me aware of my errors, and, supposing that I had reached some satisfactory conclusion, in bringing others to a fuller understanding of my speculations ; and, as many can see more than can a single man, they might help in leading others who from the present time may begin to avail themselves of my system, to assist me likewise with their discoveries. But though I recognise that I am extremely liable to err, and though I almost never trust the first reflections that I arrive at, the experience which I have had of the objections which may be made to my system prevents my having any hope of deriving profit from them. For I have often had experience of the judgments both of those whom I have esteemed as my friends, and of some others to whom I believed myself to be indifferent, and even, too, of some whose ill-feeling and envy would, I felt sure, make them endeavour to reveal what affection concealed from the eyes of my friends. But rarely has it happened that any objection has been made which I did not in some sort foresee, unless where it was something very far removed from my subject. In this way hardly ever have I encountered any censor of my opinions who did not appear to me to be either less rigorous or less judicial than myself. And I certainly never remarked that by means of disputations employed by the Schools any truth has been discovered of which we were formerly ignorant. And so long as each side attempts to vanquish his opponent, there is a much more serious attempt to establish probability than to weigh the reasons on either side ; and those who have for long been excellent pleaders are not for that reason the best judges.

As to the advantage which others may receive from the communication of my reflections, it could not be very great, inasmuch as I have not yet carried them so far as that it is not necessary to add many things before they can be brought into practice. And I think I can without vanity say that if anyone is capable of doing this, it should be myself rather than another—not indeed that there may not be in the world many minds incomparably superior to my own, but because no one can so well understand a thing and make it his own when learnt from another as when it is discovered for himself. As regards the matter in hand there is so much truth in this, that although I have often explained some of my opinions to persons of very good intelligence, who, while I talked to them appeared to understand them very clearly, yet when they recounted them I remarked that they had almost always altered them in such a manner that I could no longer acknowledge them as mine. On this account I am very glad to have the opportunity here of begging my descendants never to believe that what is told to them proceeded from myself unless I have myself divulged it. And I do not in the least wonder at the extravagances attributed to all the ancient philosophers whose writings we do not possess, nor do I judge from these that their thoughts were very unreasonable, considering that theirs were the best minds of the time they lived in, but only that they have been imperfectly represented to us. We see, too, that it hardly ever happens that any of their disciples surpassed them, and I am sure that those who most passionately follow Aristotle now-a-days would think themselves happy if they had as much knowledge of nature as he had, even if this were on the condition that they should never attain to any more. They are like the ivy that never tries to mount above the trees which give it support, and which often even descends again after it has reached their summit; for it appears to me that such men also sink again—that is to say, somehow render themselves more ignorant than they would have been had they abstained from study altogether. For, not content with knowing all that is intelligibly explained in their author, they wish in addition to find in him the solution of many difficulties of which he says nothing, and in regard to which he possibly had no thought at all. At the same time their mode of philosophising is very convenient for those who have abilities of a very mediocre kind, for the obscurity of the distinctions and principles of which they make use, is the reason of their being able to talk of all things as boldly as though they really knew about them, and defend all that they say against the most subtle and acute, without any one having the means of convincing them to the contrary. In this they seem to me like a blind man who, in order to fight on equal terms with one who sees, would have the latter to come into the bottom of a very dark cave. I may say, too, that it is in the interest of such people that I should abstain from publishing the principles of philosophy of which I make use, for, being so simple and evident as they are, I should, in publishing them, do the same as though I threw open the windows and caused daylight to enter the cave into which they have descended in order to fight. But even the best minds have no reason to desire to be acquainted with these principles, for if they wish to be able to talk of everything and acquire a reputation for learning, they will more readily attain their end by contenting themselves with the appearance of truth which may be found in all sorts of things without much trouble, than in seeking for truth which only reveals itself little by little in certain spheres, and which, when others come into question, obliges one to confess one's ignorance. If, however, they prefer the knowledge of some small amount of truth to the vanity of seeming to be ignorant of nothing, which knowledge is doubtless preferable, or if they desire to follow a course similar to my own, it is not necessary that I should say any more than what I have already said in this Discourse. For if they are capable of passing beyond the point I have reached, they will also so much the more be able to find by themselves all that I believe myself to have discovered; since, not having examined anything but in its order, it is certain that what remains for me to discover is in itself more difficult and more recondite than anything that I have hitherto been able to meet with, and they would have much less pleasure in learning from me than from themselves. Besides, the habit which they will acquire of seeking first things that are simple and then little by little and by degrees passing to others more difficult, will be of more use than could be all my instructions. For, as regards myself, I am persuaded that if from my youth up I had been taught all the truths of which I have since sought the demonstrations, or if I had not had any difficulty in learning them, I should perhaps never have known any others, or at least I should never have acquired the habit or facility which I think I have obtained, of ever finding them anew, in proportion as I set myself to seek for them. And, in a word, if there is any work at all which cannot be so well achieved by another as by him who has begun it, it is that at which I labour.

It is true as regards the experiments which may conduce to this end, that one man could not possibly accomplish all of them. But yet he could not, to good advantage, employ other hands than his own, excepting those of artisans or persons of that kind whom he could pay, and whom the hope of gain—which is a very effectual incentive—might cause to perform with exactitude all the things they were directed to accomplish. As to those who, whether by curiosity or desire to learn, might possibly offer him their voluntary assistance, not only are they usually more ready with promises than with performance, planning out fine sounding projects, none of which are ever realised, but they will also infallibly demand payment for their trouble by requesting the explanation of certain difficulties, or at least by empty compliments and useless talk, which could not occupy any of the student's time without causing it to be lost. And as to the experiments already made by others, even if they desired to communicate these to him—which those who term them secrets would never do—they are for the most part accompanied by so many circumstances or superfluous matter, that it would be very difficult for him to disentangle the truth. In addition to this he would find nearly all so badly explained, or even so false (because those who carried them out were forced to make them appear to be in conformity with their principles), that if there had been some which might have been of use to him, they would hardly be worth the time that would be required in making the selection. So true is this, that if there were anywhere in the world a person whom one knew to be assuredly capable of discovering matters of the highest importance and those of the greatest possible utility to the public, and if for this reason all other men were eager by every means in their power to help him in reaching the end which he set before him, I do not see that they could do anything for him beyond contributing to defray the expenses of the experiments which might be requisite, or, for the rest, seeing that he was not deprived of his leisure by the importunities of anyone. But, in addition to the fact that I neither esteem myself so highly as to be willing to promise anything extraordinary, nor give scope to an imagination so vain as to conceive that the public should interest itself greatly in my designs, I do not yet own a soul so base as to be willing to accept from anyone whatever a favour which it might be supposed I did not merit.

All those considerations taken together were, three years ago, the cause of my not desiring to publish the Treatise which I had on hand, and the reason why I even formed the resolution of not bringing to light during my life any other of so general a kind, or one by which the foundations of Physics could be understood. But since then two other reasons came into operation which compelled me to bring forward certain attempts, as I have done here, and to render to the public some account of my actions and designs. The first is that if I failed to do so, many who knew the intention I formerly had of publishing certain writings, might imagine that the causes for which I abstained from so doing were more to my disadvantage than they really were ; for although I do not care immoderately for glory, or, if I dare say so, although I even hate it, inasmuch as I judge it to be antagonistic to the repose which I esteem above all other things, at the same time I never tried to conceal my actions as though they were crimes, nor have I used many precautions against being known, partly because I should have thought it damaging to myself, and partly because it would have given me a sort of disquietude which would again have militated against the perfect repose of spirit which I seek. And forasmuch as having in this way always held myself in a condition of indifference as

regards whether I was known or was not known, I have not yet
been able to prevent myself from acquiring some sort of reputation,
I thought that I should do my best at least to prevent myself from
acquiring an evil reputation.   The other reason which obliged me
to put this in writing is that I am becoming every day more and
more alive to the delay which is being suffered in the design which
I have of instructing myself, because of the lack of an infinitude of
experiments, which it is impossible that I should perform without
the aid of others : and although I do not flatter myself so much as
to hope that the public should to any large degree participate in my
interest, I yet do not wish to be found wanting, both on my own
account, and as one day giving occasion to those who will survive
me of reproaching me for the fact that I might have left many
matters in a much better condition than I have done, had I not too
much neglected to make them understand in what way they could
have contributed to the accomplishment of my designs.

And I thought that it was easy for me to select certain matters
which would not be the occasion for many controversies, nor yet
oblige me to propound more of my principles than I wish, and
which yet would suffice to allow a pretty clear manifestation of what
I can do and what I cannot do in the sciences.   In this I cannot
say whether I have succeeded or have not succeeded, and I do not
wish to anticipate the judgment of any one by myself speaking of
my writings ; but I shall be very glad if they will examine them.
And in order that they may have the better opportunity of so
doing, I beg all those who have any objections to offer to take the
trouble of sending them to my publishers, so that, being made
aware of them, I may try at the same time to subjoin my reply.   By
this means, the reader, seeing objections and reply at the same
time, will the more easily judge of the truth ; for I do not promise
in any instance to make lengthy replies, but just to avow my errors
very frankly if I am convinced of them ; or, if I cannot perceive
them, to say simply what I think requisite for the defence of the
matters I have written, without adding the exposition of any new
matter, so that I may not be endlessly engaged in passing from one
side to the other.

If some of the matters of which I spoke in the beginning of the
Dioptrics and *Meteors* should at first sight give offence because
I call them hypotheses and do not appear to care about their proof,
let them have the patience to read these in entirety, and I hope
that they will find themselves satisfied.   For it appears to me that

the reasonings are so mutually interwoven, that as the later ones are demonstrated by the earlier, which are their causes, the earlier are reciprocally demonstrated by the later which are their effects. And it must not be imagined that in this I commit the fallacy which logicians name arguing in a circle, for, since experience renders the greater part of these effects very certain, the causes from which I deduce them do not so much serve to prove their existence as to explain them ; on the other hand, the causes are explained by the effects. And I have not named them hypotheses with any other object than that it may be known that while I consider myself able to deduce them from the primary truths which I explained above, yet I particularly desired not to do so, in order that certain persons may not for this reason take occasion to build up some extravagant philosophic system on what they take to be my principles, and thus cause the blame to be put on me. I refer to those who imagine that in one day they may discover all that another has arrived at in twenty years of work, so soon as he has merely spoken to them two or three words on the subject; while they are really all the more subject to err, and less capable of perceiving the truth as they are the more subtle and lively. For as regards the opinions that are truly mine I do not apologise for them as being new, inasmuch as if we consider the reasons of them well, I assure myself that they will be found to be so simple and so conformable to common sense, as to appear less extraordinary and less paradoxical than any others which may be held on similar subjects. And I do not even boast of being the first discoverer of any of them, but only state that I have adopted them, not because they have been held by others, nor because they have not been so held, but only because Reason has persuaded me of their truth.

Even if artisans are not at once able to carry out the invention[1] explained in the *Dioptrics*, I do not for that reason think that it can be said that it is to be condemned ; for, inasmuch as great address and practice is required to make and adjust the mechanism which I have described without omitting any detail, I should not be less astonished at their succeeding at the first effort than I should be supposing some one were in one day to learn to play the guitar with skill, just because a good sheet of musical notation were set up before him. And if I write in French which is the language of my country, rather than in Latin which is that of my teachers, that is

[1] Doubtless the machine for the purpose of cutting lenses which Descartes so minutely describes.

because I hope that those who avail themselves only of their natural reason in its purity may be better judges of my opinions than those who believe only in the writings of the ancients; and as to those who unite good sense with study, whom alone I crave for my judges, they will not, I feel sure, be so partial to Latin as to refuse to follow my reasoning because I expound it in a vulgar tongue.

For the rest, I do not desire to speak here more particularly of the progress which I hope in the future to make in the sciences, nor to bind myself as regards the public with any promise which I shall not with certainty be able to fulfil. But I will just say that I have resolved not to employ the time which remains to me in life in any other matter than in endeavouring to acquire some knowledge of nature, which shall be of such a kind that it will enable us to arrive at rules for Medicine more assured than those which have as yet been attained; and my inclination is so strongly opposed to any other kind of pursuit, more especially to those which can only be useful to some by being harmful to others, that if certain circumstances had constrained me to employ them, I do not think that I should have been capable of succeeding. In so saying I make a declaration that I know very well cannot help me to make myself of consideration in the world, but to this end I have no desire to attain; and I shall always hold myself to be more indebted to those by whose favour I may enjoy my leisure without hindrance, than I shall be to any who may offer me the most honourable position in all the world.

MEDITATIONS ON
FIRST PHILOSOPHY

TO THE MOST WISE AND ILLUSTRIOUS THE DEAN AND DOCTORS OF THE SACRED FACULTY OF THEOLOGY IN PARIS.

The motive which induces me to present to you this Treatise is so excellent, and, when you become' acquainted with its design, I am convinced that you will also have so excellent a motive for taking it under your protection, that I feel that I cannot do better, in order to render it in some sort acceptable to you, than in a few words to state what I have set myself to do.

I have always considered that the two questions respecting God and the Soul were the chief of those that ought to be demonstrated by philosophical rather than theological argument. For although it is quite enough for us faithful ones to accept by means of faith the fact that the human soul does not perish with the body, and that God exists, it certainly does not seem possible ever to persuade infidels of any religion, indeed, we may almost say, of any moral virtue, unless, to begin with, we prove these two facts by means of the natural reason. And inasmuch as often in this life greater rewards are offered for vice than for virtue, few people would prefer the right to the useful, were they restrained neither by the fear of God nor the expectation of another life; and although it is absolutely true that we must believe that there is a God, because we are so taught in the Holy Scriptures, and, on the other hand, that we must believe the Holy Scriptures because they come from God (the reason of this is, that, faith being a gift of God, He who gives the grace to cause us to believe other things can likewise give it to cause us to believe that He exists), we nevertheless could not place this argument before infidels, who might accuse us of reasoning in a circle. And, in truth, I have noticed that you, along with all the theologians, did not only affirm that the existence of God may be proved by the natural reason, but also that it may be inferred

55

from the Holy Scriptures, that knowledge about Him is much clearer than that which we have of many created things, and, as a matter of fact, is so easy to acquire, that those who have it not are culpable in their ignorance. This indeed appears from the Wisdom of Solomon, chapter xiii., where is is said '*Howbeit they are not to be excused; for if their understanding was so great that they could discern the world and the creatures, why did they not rather find out the Lord thereof?*' and in Romans, chapter i., it is said that they are '*without excuse*'; and again in the same place, by these words '*that which may be known of God is manifest in them,*' it seems as though we were shown that all that which can be known of God may be made manifest by means which are not derived from anywhere but from ourselves, and from the simple consideration of the nature of our minds. Hence I thought it not beside my purpose to inquire how this is so, and how God may be more easily and certainly known than the things of the world.

And as regards the soul, although many have considered that it is not easy to know its nature, and some have even dared to say that human reasons have convinced us that it would perish with the body, and that faith alone could believe the contrary, nevertheless, inasmuch as the Lateran Council held under Leo X (in the eighth session) condemns these tenets, and as Leo expressly ordains Christian philosophers to refute their arguments and to employ all their powers in making known the truth, I have ventured in this treatise to undertake the same task.

More than that, I am aware that the principal reason which causes many impious persons not to desire to believe that there is a God, and that the human soul is distinct from the body, is that they declare that hitherto no one has been able to demonstrate these two facts; and although I am not of their opinion but, on the contrary, hold that the greater part of the reasons which have been brought forward concerning these two questions by so many great men are, when they are rightly understood, equal to so many demonstrations, and that it is almost impossible to invent new ones, it is yet in my opinion the case that nothing more useful can be accomplished in philosophy than once for all to seek with care for the best of these reasons, and to set them forth in so clear and exact a manner, that it will henceforth be evident to everybody that they are veritable demonstrations. And, finally, inasmuch as it was desired that I should undertake this task by many who were aware that I had cultivated a certain Method for the resolution of difficulties of every kind in the Sciences—a method which it is true is not novel, since there is nothing more ancient than the truth, but of which they were aware that I had made use successfully enough in other matters of difficulty—I have thought that it was my duty also to make trial of it in the present matter.

Now all that I could accomplish in the matter is contained in this Treatise. Not that I have here drawn together all the different reasons which might be brought forward to serve as proofs of this subject: for that never seemed to be necessary excepting when there was no one single proof that was certain. But I have treated the first and principal ones in such a manner that I can venture to bring them forward as very evident and very certain demonstrations. And more than that, I will say that these proofs are such that I do not think that there is any way open to the human mind by which it can ever succeed in discovering better. For the importance of the subject, and the glory of God to which all this relates, constrain me to speak here somewhat more freely of myself than is my habit. Nevertheless, whatever certainty and evidence I find in my reasons, I cannot persuade myself that all the world is capable of understanding them. Still, just as in Geometry there are many demonstrations that have been left to us by Archimedes, by Apollonius, by Pappus, and others, which are accepted by everyone as perfectly certain and evident (because they clearly contain nothing which, considered by itself, is not very easy to understand, and as all through that which follows has an exact connection with, and dependence on that which precedes), nevertheless, because they are somewhat lengthy, and demand a mind wholly devoted to their consideration, they are only taken in and understood by a very limited number of persons. Similarly, although I judge that those of which I here make use are equal to, or even surpass in certainty and evidence, the demonstrations of Geometry, I yet apprehend that they cannot be adequately understood by many, both because they are also a little lengthy and dependent the one on the other, and principally because they demand a mind wholly free of prejudices, and one which can be easily detached from the affairs of the senses. And, truth to say, there are not so many in the world who are fitted for metaphysical speculations as there are for those of Geometry. And more than that; there is still this difference, that in Geometry, since each one is persuaded that nothing must be advanced of which there is not a certain demonstration, those who are not entirely adepts more frequently err in approving what is false, in order to give the impression that they understand it, than in refuting the true. But the case is different in philosophy where everyone believes that all is problematical, and few give themselves to the search after truth; and the greater number, in their desire to acquire a reputation for boldness of thought, arrogantly combat the most important of truths[1].

That is why, whatever force there may be in my reasonings, seeing they belong to philosophy, I cannot hope that they will have much effect on the minds of men, unless you extend to them your protection. But the estimation in which your Company is universally held is so great, and the name of SORBONNE carries with it so much authority, that, next to the Sacred Councils, never has such deference been paid to the judgment of any Body, not only in what concerns the faith, but also in what regards human philosophy as well : everyone indeed believes that it is not possible to discover elsewhere more perspicacity and solidity, or more integrity and wisdom in pronouncing judgment. For this reason I have no doubt that if you deign to take the trouble in the first place of correcting this work (for being conscious not only of my infirmity, but also of my ignorance, I should not dare to state that it was free from errors), and then, after adding to it these things that are lacking to it, completing those which are imperfect, and yourselves taking the trouble to give a more ample explanation of those things which have need of it, or at least making me aware of the defects so that I may apply myself to remedy them[1]—when this is done and when finally the reasonings by which I prove that there is a God, and that the human soul differs from the body, shall be carried to that point of perspicuity to which I am sure they can be carried in order that they may be esteemed as perfectly exact demonstrations, if you deign to authorise your approbation and to render public testimony to their truth and certainty, I do not doubt, I say, that henceforward all the errors and false opinions which have ever existed regarding these two questions will soon be effaced from the minds of men. For the truth itself will easily cause all men of mind and learning to subscribe to your judgment ; and your authority will cause the atheists, who are usually more arrogant than learned or judicious, to rid themselves of their spirit of contradiction or lead them possibly themselves to defend the reasonings which they find being received as demonstrations by all persons of

---

[1] The French version is followed here.

consideration, lest they appear not to understand them. And, finally, all others will easily yield to such a mass of evidence, and there will be none who dares to doubt the existence of God and the real and true distinction between the human soul and the body. It is for you now in your singular wisdom to judge of the importance of the establishment of such beliefs [you who see the disorders produced by the doubt of them][1]. But it would not become me to say more in consideration of the cause of God and religion to those who have always been the most worthy supports of the Catholic Church.

PREFACE TO THE READER.

I have already slightly touched on these two questions of God and the human soul in the Discourse on the Method of rightly conducting the Reason and seeking truth in the Sciences, published in French in the year 1637. Not that I had the design of treating these with any thoroughness, but only so to speak in passing, and in order to ascertain by the judgment of the readers how I should treat them later on. For these questions have always appeared to me to be of such importance that I judged it suitable to speak of them more than once ; and the road which I follow in the explanation of them is so little trodden, and so far removed from the ordinary path, that I did not judge it to be expedient to set it forth at length in French and in a Discourse which might be read by everyone, in case the feebler minds should believe that it was permitted to them to attempt to follow the same path.

But, having in this Discourse on Method begged all those who have found in my writings somewhat deserving of censure to do me the favour of acquainting me with the grounds of it, nothing worthy of remark has been objected to in them beyond two matters : to these two I wish here to reply in a few words before undertaking their more detailed discussion.

The first objection is that it does not follow from the fact that the human mind reflecting on itself does not perceive itself to be other than a thing that thinks, that its nature or its essence consists only in its being a thing that thinks, in the sense that this word *only* excludes all other things which might also be supposed to pertain to the nature of the soul. To this objection I reply that it was not my intention in that place to exclude these in accordance with the order that looks to the truth of the matter (as to which

---

[1] When it is thought desirable to insert additional readings from the French version this will be indicated by the use of square brackets.

I was not then dealing), but only in accordance with the order of
my thought [perception]; thus my meaning was that so far as
I was aware, I knew nothing clearly as belonging to my essence,
excepting that I was a thing that thinks, or a thing that has in
itself the faculty of thinking. But I shall show hereafter how from
the fact that I know no other thing which pertains to my essence, it
follows that there is no other thing which really does belong to it.

The second objection is that it does not follow from the fact
that I have in myself the idea of something more perfect than I am,
that this idea is more perfect than I, and much less that what is
represented by this idea exists. But I reply that in this term *idea*
there is here something equivocal, for it may either be taken
materially, as an act of my understanding, and in this sense it
cannot be said that it is more perfect than I; or it may be taken
objectively, as the thing which is represented by this act, which,
although we do not suppose it to exist outside of my understanding,
may, none the less, be more perfect than I, because of its essence.
And in following out this Treatise I shall show more fully how,
from the sole fact that I have in myself the idea of a thing more
perfect than myself, it follows that this thing truly exists.

In addition to these two objections I have also seen two fairly
lengthy works on this subject, which, however, did not so much im-
pugn my reasonings as my conclusions, and this by arguments drawn
from the ordinary atheistic sources. But, because such arguments
cannot make any impression on the minds of those who really
understand my reasonings, and as the judgments of many are so
feeble and irrational that they very often allow themselves to be
persuaded by the opinions which they have first formed, however
false and far removed from reason they may be, rather than by a
true and solid but subsequently received refutation of these opinions,
I do not desire to reply here to their criticisms in case of being first
of all obliged to state them. I shall only say in general that all
that is said by the atheist against the existence of God, always
depends either on the fact that we ascribe to God affections which
are human, or that we attribute so much strength and wisdom to
our minds that we even have the presumption to desire to determine
and understand that which God can and ought to do. In this
way all that they allege will cause us no difficulty, provided only
we remember that we must consider our minds as things which are
finite and limited, and God as a Being who is incomprehensible and
infinite.

Now that I have once for all recognised and acknowledged the opinions of men, I at once begin to treat of God and the human soul, and at the same time to treat of the whole of the First Philosophy, without however expecting any praise from the vulgar and without the hope that my book will have many readers. On the contrary, I should never advise anyone to read it excepting those who desire to meditate seriously with me, and who can detach their minds from affairs of sense, and deliver themselves entirely from every sort of prejudice. I know too well that such men exist in a very small number. But for those who, without caring to comprehend the order and connections of my reasonings, form their criticisms on detached portions arbitrarily selected, as is the custom with many, these, I say, will not obtain much profit from reading this Treatise. And although they perhaps in several parts find occasion of cavilling, they can for all their pains make no objection which is urgent or deserving of reply.

And inasmuch as I make no promise to others to satisfy them at once, and as I do not presume so much on my own powers as to believe myself capable of foreseeing all that can cause difficulty to anyone, I shall first of all set forth in these Meditations the very considerations by which I persuade myself that I have reached a certain and evident knowledge of the truth, in order to see if, by the same reasons which persuaded me, I can also persuade others. And, after that, I shall reply to the objections which have been made to me by persons of genius and learning to whom I have sent my Meditations for examination, before submitting them to the press. For they have made so many objections and these so different, that I venture to promise that it will be difficult for anyone to bring to mind criticisms of any consequence which have not been already touched upon. This is why I beg those who read these Meditations to form no judgment upon them unless they have given themselves the trouble to read all the objections as well as the replies which I have made to them[1].

---

[1] Between the *Præfatio ad Lectorem* and the *Synopsis*, the Paris Edition (1st Edition) interpolates an *Index* which is not found in the Amsterdam Edition (2nd Edition). Since Descartes did not reproduce it, he was doubtless not its author. Mersenne probably composed it himself, adjusting it to the paging of the first Edition.

(Note in Adam and Tannery's Edition.)

SYNOPSIS OF THE SIX FOLLOWING MEDITATIONS.

In the first Meditation I set forth the reasons for which we may, generally speaking, doubt about all things and especially about material things, at least so long as we have no other foundations for the sciences than those which we have hitherto possessed. But although the utility of a Doubt which is so general does not at first appear, it is at the same time very great, inasmuch as it delivers us from every kind of prejudice, and sets out for us a very simple way by which the mind may detach itself from the senses; and finally it makes it impossible for us ever to doubt those things which we have once discovered to be true.

In the second Meditation, mind, which making use of the liberty which pertains to it, takes for granted that all those things of whose existence it has the least doubt, are non-existent, recognises that it is however absolutely impossible that it does not itself exist. This point is likewise of the greatest moment, inasmuch as by this means a distinction is easily drawn between the things which pertain to mind —that is to say to the intellectual nature—and those which pertain to body.

But because it may be that some expect from me in this place a statement of the reasons establishing the immortality of the soul, I feel that I should here make known to them that having aimed at writing nothing in all this Treatise of which I do not possess very exact demonstrations, I am obliged to follow a similar order to that made use of by the geometers, which is to begin by putting forward as premises all those things upon which the proposition that we seek depends, before coming to any conclusion regarding it. Now the first and principal matter which is requisite for thoroughly under-standing the immortality of the soul is to form the clearest possible conception of it, and one which will be entirely distinct from all the conceptions which we may have of body; and in this Medita-tion this has been done. In addition to this it is requisite that we may be assured that all the things which we conceive clearly and distinctly are true in the very way in which we think them; and this could not be proved previously to the Fourth Meditation. Further we must have a distinct conception of corporeal nature, which is given partly in this Second, and partly in the Fifth and Sixth Meditations. And finally we should conclude from all this, that those things which we conceive clearly and distinctly as being diverse substances, as we regard mind and body to be, are really substances essentially distinct one from the other; and this is the conclusion of the Sixth Meditation. This is further confirmed in this same Meditation by the fact that we cannot conceive of body excepting in so far as it is divisible, while the mind cannot be conceived of excepting as indivisible. For we are not able to conceive of the half of a mind as we can do of the smallest of all bodies; so that we see that not only are their natures different but even in some respects contrary to one another. I have not however dealt further with this matter in this treatise, both because what I have said is sufficient to show clearly enough that the extinction of the mind does not follow from the corruption of the body, and also to give men the hope of another life after death, as also because the premises from which the immortality of the soul may be deduced depend on an elucidation of a complete system of Physics. This would mean to establish in the first place that all substances generally—that is to say all things which cannot exist without being created by God—are in their nature incorruptible, and that they can never cease to exist unless God, in denying to them his concurrence, reduce them to nought; and secondly that body, regarded generally, is a substance, which is the reason why it also cannot perish, but that the human body, inasmuch as it differs from other bodies, is composed only of a certain configuration of members and of other similar accidents, while the human mind is not similarly composed of any accidents, but is a pure substance. For although all the accidents of mind be changed, although, for instance, it think certain things, will others, perceive others, etc., despite all this it does not emerge from these changes another mind: the human body on the other hand becomes a different thing from the sole fact that the figure or form of any of its portions is found to be changed. From this it follows that the human body may indeed easily enough perish, but the mind [or soul of man (I make no distinction between them)] is owing to its nature immortal.

In the third Meditation it seems to me that I have explained at sufficient length the principal argument of which I make use in order to prove the existence of God. But none the less, because I did not wish in that place to make use of any comparisons derived from corporeal things, so as to withdraw as much as I could the minds of readers from the senses, there may perhaps have remained many obscurities which, however, will, I hope, be entirely removed by the Replies which I have made to the Objections which have been set before me. Amongst others there is, for example, this one, 'How the idea in

*us of a being supremely perfect possesses so much objective reality
[that is to say participates by representation in so many degrees of
being and perfection] that it necessarily proceeds from a cause which
is absolutely perfect.   This is illustrated in these Replies by the
comparison of a very perfect machine, the idea of which is found in
the mind of some workman.   For as the objective contrivance of this
idea must have some cause, i.e. either the science of the workman or
that of some other from whom he has received the idea, it is similarly
impossible that the idea of God which is in us should not have God
himself as its cause.*

*In the fourth Meditation it is shown that all these things which
we very clearly and distinctly perceive are true, and at the same time
it is explained in what the nature of error or falsity consists.   This
must of necessity be known both for the confirmation of the preceding truths and for the better comprehension of those that follow.
(But it must meanwhile be remarked that I do not in any way there
treat of sin—that is to say of the error which is committed in the
pursuit of good and evil, but only of that which arises in the deciding
between the true and the false.   And I do not intend to speak of
matters pertaining to the Faith or the conduct of life, but only of
those which concern speculative truths, and which may be known by
the sole aid of the light of nature.)*

*In the fifth Meditation corporeal nature generally is explained,
and in addition to this the existence of God is demonstrated by a
new proof in which there may possibly be certain difficulties also, but
the solution of these will be seen in the Replies to the Objections.
And further I show in what sense it is true to say that the certainty
of geometrical demonstrations is itself dependent on the knowledge
of God.*

*Finally in the Sixth I distinguish the action of the under-
standing[1] from that of the imagination[2]; the marks by which this
distinction is made are described.   I here show that the mind of man
is really distinct from the body, and at the same time that the two
are so closely joined together that they form, so to speak, a single
thing.   All the errors which proceed from the senses are then
surveyed, while the means of avoiding them are demonstrated, and
finally all the reasons from which we may deduce the existence of
material things are set forth.   Not that I judge them to be very
useful in establishing that which they prove, to wit, that there is in*

---

[1] *intellectio.*   [2] *imaginatio.*

truth a world, that men possess bodies, and other such things which never have been doubted by anyone of sense; but because in considering these closely we come to see that they are neither so strong nor so evident as those arguments which lead us to the knowledge of our mind and of God; so that these last must be the most certain and most evident facts which can fall within the cognizance of the human mind.   And this is the whole matter that I have tried to prove in these Meditations, for which reason I here omit to speak of many other questions with which I dealt incidentally in this discussion.

MEDITATIONS ON THE FIRST PHILOSOPHY IN WHICH THE EXISTENCE OF GOD AND THE DISTINCTION BETWEEN MIND AND BODY ARE DEMONSTRATED[1].

MEDITATION I.

Of the things which may be brought within the sphere of the doubtful.

It is now some years since I detected how many were the false beliefs that I had from my earliest youth admitted as true, and how doubtful was everything I had since constructed on this basis ; and from that time I was convinced that I must once for all seriously undertake to rid myself of all the opinions which I had formerly accepted, and commence to build anew from the foundation, if I wanted to establish any firm and permanent structure in the sciences. But as this enterprise appeared to be a very great one, I waited until I had attained an age so mature that I could not hope that at any later date I should be better fitted to execute my design. This reason caused me to delay so long that I should feel that I was doing wrong were I to occupy in deliberation the time that yet remains to me for action. To-day, then, since very opportunely for the plan I have in view I have delivered my mind from every care [and am happily agitated by no passions] and since I have procured for myself an assured leisure in a peaceable retirement, I shall at last seriously and freely address myself to the general upheaval of all my former opinions.

[1] In place of this long title at the head of the page the first Edition had immediately after the Synopsis, and on the same page 7, simply 'First Meditation.' (Adam's Edition.)

Now for this object it is not necessary that I should show that all of these are false—I shall perhaps never arrive at this end. But inasmuch as reason already persuades me that I ought no less carefully to withhold my assent from matters which are not entirely certain and indubitable than from those which appear to me manifestly to be false, if I am able to find in each one some reason to doubt, this will suffice to justify my rejecting the whole. And for that end it will not be requisite that I should examine each in particular, which would be an endless undertaking; for owing to the fact that the destruction of the foundations of necessity brings with it the downfall of the rest of the edifice, I shall only in the first place attack those principles upon which all my former opinions rested.

All that up to the present time I have accepted as most true and certain I have learned either from the senses or through the senses; but it is sometimes proved to me that these senses are deceptive, and it is wiser not to trust entirely to any thing by which we have once been deceived.

But it may be that although the senses sometimes deceive us concerning things which are hardly perceptible, or very far away, there are yet many others to be met with as to which we cannot reasonably have any doubt, although we recognise them by their means. For example, there is the fact that I am here, seated by the fire, attired in a dressing gown, having this paper in my hands and other similar matters. And how could I deny that these hands and this body are mine, were it not perhaps that I compare myself to certain persons, devoid of sense, whose cerebella are so troubled and clouded by the violent vapours of black bile, that they constantly assure us that they think they are kings when they are really quite poor, or that they are clothed in purple when they are really without covering, or who imagine that they have an earthenware head or are nothing but pumpkins or are made of glass. But they are mad, and I should not be any the less insane were I to follow examples so extravagant.

At the same time I must remember that I am a man, and that consequently I am in the habit of sleeping, and in my dreams representing to myself the same things or sometimes even less probable things, than do those who are insane in their waking moments. How often has it happened to me that in the night I dreamt that I found myself in this particular place, that I was dressed and seated near the fire, whilst in reality I was lying undressed in bed! At this moment it does indeed seem to me that it is with eyes awake that I am looking at this paper; that this head which I move is not asleep, that it is deliberately and of set purpose that I extend my hand and perceive it; what happens in sleep does not appear so clear nor so distinct as does all this. But in thinking over this I remind myself that on many occasions I have in sleep been deceived by similar illusions, and in dwelling carefully on this reflection I see so manifestly that there are no certain indications by which we may clearly distinguish wakefulness from sleep that I am lost in astonishment. And my astonishment is such that it is almost capable of persuading me that I now dream.

Now let us assume that we are asleep and that all these particulars, e.g. that we open our eyes, shake our head, extend our hands, and so on, are but false delusions; and let us reflect that possibly neither our hands nor our whole body are such as they appear to us to be. At the same time we must at least confess that the things which are represented to us in sleep are like painted representations which can only have been formed as the counterparts of something real and true, and that in this way those general things at least, i.e. eyes, a head, hands, and a whole body, are not imaginary things, but things really existent. For, as a matter of fact, painters, even when they study with the greatest skill to represent sirens and satyrs by forms the most strange and extraordinary, cannot give them natures which are entirely new, but merely make a certain medley of the members of different animals; or if their imagination is extravagant enough to invent something so novel that nothing similar has ever before been seen, and that then their work represents a thing purely fictitious and absolutely false, it is certain all the same that the colours of which this is composed are necessarily real. And for the same reason, although these general things, to wit, [a body], eyes, a head, hands, and such like, may be imaginary, we are bound at the same time to confess that there are at least some other objects yet more simple and more universal, which are real and true; and of these just in the same way as with certain real colours, all these images of things which dwell in our thoughts, whether true and real or false and fantastic, are formed.

To such a class of things pertains corporeal nature in general, and its extension, the figure of extended things, their quantity or magnitude and number, as also the place in which they are, the time which measures their duration, and so on.

That is possibly why our reasoning is not unjust when we conclude from this that Physics, Astronomy, Medicine and all other sciences which have as their end the consideration of composite things, are very dubious and uncertain; but that Arithmetic, Geometry and other sciences of that kind which only treat of things that are very simple and very general, without taking great trouble to ascertain whether they are actually existent or not, contain some measure of certainty and an element of the indubitable. For whether I am awake or asleep, two and three together always form five, and the square can never have more than four sides, and it does not seem possible that truths so clear and apparent can be suspected of any falsity [or uncertainty].

Nevertheless I have long had fixed in my mind the belief that an all-powerful God existed by whom I have been created such as I am. But how do I know that He has not brought it to pass that there is no earth, no heaven, no extended body, no magnitude, no place, and that nevertheless [I possess the perceptions of all these things and that] they seem to me to exist just exactly as I now see them? And, besides, as I sometimes imagine that others deceive themselves in the things which they think they know best, how do I know that I am not deceived every time that I add two and three, or count the sides of a square, or judge of things yet simpler, if anything simpler can be imagined? But possibly God has not desired that I should be thus deceived, for He is said to be supremely good. If, however, it is contrary to His goodness to have made me such that I constantly deceive myself, it would also appear to be contrary to His goodness to permit me to be sometimes deceived, and nevertheless I cannot doubt that He does permit this.

There may indeed be those who would prefer to deny the existence of a God so powerful, rather than believe that all other things are uncertain. But let us not oppose them for the present, and grant that all that is here said of a God is a fable; nevertheless in whatever way they suppose that I have arrived at the state of being that I have reached—whether they attribute it to fate or to accident, or make out that it is by a continual succession of antecedents, or by some other method—since to err and deceive oneself is a defect, it is clear that the greater will be the probability of my being so imperfect as to deceive myself ever, as is the Author to whom they assign my origin the less powerful. To these reasons I have certainly nothing to reply, but at the end I feel constrained to confess that there is nothing in all that I formerly believed to be

true, of which I cannot in some measure doubt, and that not merely
through want of thought or through levity, but for reasons which
are very powerful and maturely considered; so that henceforth
I ought not the less carefully to refrain from giving credence to
these opinions than to that which is manifestly false, if I desire to
arrive at any certainty [in the sciences].

But it is not sufficient to have made these remarks, we must
also be careful to keep them in mind. For these ancient and
commonly held opinions still revert frequently to my mind, long
and familiar custom having given them the right to occupy my
mind against my inclination and rendered them almost masters of
my belief; nor will I ever lose the habit of deferring to them or of
placing my confidence in them, so long as I consider them as they
really are, i.e. opinions in some measure doubtful, as I have just
shown, and at the same time highly probable, so that there is much
more reason to believe in than to deny them. That is why I
consider that I shall not be acting amiss, if, taking of set purpose
a contrary belief, I allow myself to be deceived, and for a certain
time pretend that all these opinions are entirely false and imaginary,
until at last, having thus balanced my former prejudices with my
latter [so that they cannot divert my opinions more to one side
than to the other], my judgment will no longer be dominated by
bad usage or turned away from the right knowledge of the truth.
For I am assured that there can be neither peril nor error in this
course, and that I cannot at present yield too much to distrust,
since I am not considering the question of action, but only of
knowledge.

I shall then suppose, not that God who is supremely good and
the fountain of truth, but some evil genius not less powerful
than deceitful, has employed his whole energies in deceiving me;
I shall consider that the heavens, the earth, colours, figures, sound,
and all other external things are nought but the illusions and
dreams of which this genius has availed himself in order to lay
traps for my credulity; I shall consider myself as having no hands,
no eyes, no flesh, no blood, nor any senses, yet falsely believing
myself to possess all these things; I shall remain obstinately
attached to this idea, and if by this means it is not in my power to
arrive at the knowledge of any truth, I may at least do what is in
my power [i.e. suspend my judgment], and with firm purpose avoid
giving credence to any false thing, or being imposed upon by this
arch deceiver, however powerful and deceptive he may be. But this

Radical doubt - challenge everything

task is a laborious one, and insensibly a certain lassitude leads me
into the course of my ordinary life.   And just as a captive who in
sleep enjoys an imaginary liberty, when he begins to suspect that
his liberty is but a dream, fears to awaken, and conspires with these
agreeable illusions that the deception may be prolonged, so insensibly
of my own accord I fall back into my former opinions, and I dread
awakening from this slumber, lest the laborious wakefulness which
would follow the tranquillity of this repose should have to be spent
not in daylight, but in the excessive darkness of the difficulties
which have just been discussed.

Questioning what he knows

MEDITATION II.

*Of the Nature of the Human Mind; and that it is more easily
known than the Body.*

The Meditation of yesterday filled my mind with so many doubts
that it is no longer in my power to forget them.   And yet I do not
see in what manner I can resolve them ; and, just as if I had all of
a sudden fallen into very deep water, I am so disconcerted that
I can neither make certain of setting my feet on the bottom, nor
can I swim and so support myself on the surface.   I shall nevertheless make an effort and follow anew the same path as that on which
I yesterday entered, i.e. I shall proceed by setting aside all that in
which the least doubt could be supposed to exist, just as if I had
discovered that it was absolutely false ; and I shall ever follow in
this road until I have met with something which is certain, or at
least, if I can do nothing else, until I have learned for certain that
there is nothing in the world that is certain.   Archimedes, in order
that he might draw the terrestrial globe out of its place, and
transport it elsewhere, demanded only that one point should be
fixed and immoveable ; in the same way I shall have the right to
conceive high hopes if I am happy enough to discover one thing
only which is certain and indubitable.

I suppose, then, that all the things that I see are false ; I
persuade myself that nothing has ever existed of all that my
fallacious memory represents to me.   I consider that I possess no
senses ; I imagine that body, figure, extension, movement and place
are but the fictions of my mind.   What, then, can be esteemed as
true ?   Perhaps nothing at all, unless that there is nothing in the
world that is certain.

But how can I know there is not something different from those things that I have just considered, of which one cannot have the slightest doubt? Is there not some God, or some other being by whatever name we call it, who puts these reflections into my mind? That is not necessary, for is it not possible that I am capable of producing them myself? I myself, am I not at least something? But I have already denied that I had senses and body. Yet I hesitate, for what follows from that? Am I so dependent on body and senses that I cannot exist without these? But I was persuaded that there was nothing in all the world, that there was no heaven, no earth, that there were no minds, nor any bodies : was I not then likewise persuaded that I did not exist? Not at all; of a surety I myself did exist since I persuaded myself of something [or merely because I thought of something]. But there is some deceiver or other, very powerful and very cunning, who ever employs his ingenuity in deceiving me. Then without doubt I exist also if he deceives me, and let him deceive me as much as he will, he can never cause me to be nothing so long as I think that I am something. So that after having reflected well and carefully examined all things, we must come to the definite conclusion that this proposition : I am, I exist, is necessarily true each time that I pronounce it, or that I mentally conceive it.

But I do not yet know clearly enough what I am, I who am certain that I am; and hence I must be careful to see that I do not imprudently take some other object in place of myself, and thus that I do not go astray in respect of this knowledge that I hold to be the most certain and most evident of all that I have formerly learned. That is why I shall now consider anew what I believed myself to be before I embarked upon these last reflections; and of my former opinions I shall withdraw all that might even in a small degree be invalidated by the reasons which I have just brought forward, in order that there may be nothing at all left beyond what is absolutely certain and indubitable.

What then did I formerly believe myself to be? Undoubtedly I believed myself to be a man. But what is a man? Shall I say a reasonable animal? Certainly not; for then I should have to inquire what an animal is, and what is reasonable; and thus from a single question I should insensibly fall into an infinitude of others more difficult; and I should not wish to waste the little time and leisure remaining to me in trying to unravel subtleties like these. But I shall rather stop here to consider the thoughts which of themselves spring up in my mind, and which were not inspired by anything beyond my own nature alone when I applied myself to the consideration of my being. In the first place, then, I considered myself as having a face, hands, arms, and all that system of members composed of bones and flesh as seen in a corpse which I designated by the name of body. In addition to this I considered that I was nourished, that I walked, that I felt, and that I thought, and I referred all these actions to the soul: but I did not stop to consider what the soul was, or if I did stop, I imagined that it was something extremely rare and subtle like a wind, a flame, or an ether, which was spread throughout my grosser parts. As to body I had no manner of doubt about its nature, but thought I had a very clear knowledge of it; and if I had desired to explain it according to the notions that I had then formed of it, I should have described it thus: By the body I understand all that which can be defined by a certain figure: something which can be confined in a certain place, and which can fill a given space in such a way that every other body will be excluded from it; which can be perceived either by touch, or by sight, or by hearing, or by taste, or by smell: which can be moved in many ways not, in truth, by itself, but by something which is foreign to it, by which it is touched [and from which it receives impressions]: for to have the power of self-movement, as also of feeling or of thinking, I did not consider to appertain to the nature of body: on the contrary, I was rather astonished to find that faculties similar to them existed in some bodies.

But what am I, now that I suppose that there is a certain genius which is extremely powerful, and, if I may say so, malicious, who employs all his powers in deceiving me? Can I affirm that I possess the least of all those things which I have just said pertain to the nature of body? I pause to consider, I revolve all these things in my mind, and I find none of which I can say that it pertains to me. It would be tedious to stop to enumerate them. Let us pass to the attributes of soul and see if there is any one which is in me? What of nutrition or walking [the first mentioned]? But if it is so that I have no body it is also true that I can neither walk nor take nourishment. Another attribute is sensation. But one cannot feel without body, and besides I have thought I perceived many things during sleep that I recognised in my waking moments as not having been experienced at all. What of thinking? I find here that thought is an attribute that belongs to me; it alone cannot be separated from me. I am, I exist, that is certain. But how often? Just when I think; for it might possibly be the case if I ceased

entirely to think, that I should likewise cease altogether to exist.
I do not now admit anything which is not necessarily true : to
speak accurately I am not more than a thing which thinks, that is
to say a mind or a soul, or an understanding, or a reason, which are
terms whose significance was formerly unknown to me. I am,
however, a real thing and really exist; but what thing? I have
answered : a thing which thinks.

And what more ? I shall exercise my imagination [in order to
see if I am not something more]. I am not a collection of members
which we call the human body : I am not a subtle air distributed
through these members, I am not a wind, a fire, a vapour, a breath,
nor anything at all which I can imagine or conceive; because
I have assumed that all these were nothing. Without changing
that supposition I find that I only leave myself certain of the fact
that I am somewhat. But perhaps it is true that these same things
which I supposed were non-existent because they are unknown to
me, are really not different from the self which I know. I am not
sure about this, I shall not dispute about it now; I can only give
judgment on things that are known to me. I know that I exist,
and I inquire what I am, I whom I know to exist. But it is very
certain that the knowledge of my existence taken in its precise
significance does not depend on things whose existence is not yet
known to me; consequently it does not depend on those which
I can feign in imagination. And indeed the very term *feign* in
imagination[1] proves to me my error, for I really do this if I image
myself a something, since to imagine is nothing else than to contemplate the figure or image of a corporeal thing. But I already
know for certain that I am, and that it may be that all these images,
and, speaking generally, all things that relate to the nature of body
are nothing but dreams [and chimeras]. For this reason I see
clearly that I have as little reason to say, 'I shall stimulate my
imagination in order to know more distinctly what I am,' than if
I were to say, 'I am now awake, and I perceive somewhat that is
real and true : but because I do not yet perceive it distinctly
enough, I shall go to sleep of express purpose, so that my dreams
may represent the perception with greatest truth and evidence.'
And, thus, I know for certain that nothing of all that I can understand by means of my imagination belongs to this knowledge which
I have of myself, and that it is necessary to recall the mind from

---

[1] Or 'form an image' (effingo).

this mode of thought with the utmost diligence in order that it may be able to know its own nature with perfect distinctness.

But what then am I ? A thing which thinks. What is a thing which thinks? It is a thing which doubts, understands, [conceives], affirms, denies, wills, refuses, which also imagines and feels.

Certainly it is no small matter if all these things pertain to my nature. But why should they not so pertain? Am I not that being who now doubts nearly everything, who nevertheless understands certain things, who affirms that one only is true, who denies all the others, who desires to know more, is averse from being deceived, who imagines many things, sometimes indeed despite his will, and who perceives many likewise, as by the intervention of the bodily organs? Is there nothing in all this which is as true as it is certain that I exist, even though I should always sleep and though he who has given me being employed all his ingenuity in deceiving me? Is there likewise any one of these attributes which can be distinguished from my thought, or which might be said to be separated from myself? For it is so evident of itself that it is I who doubts, who understands, and who desires, that there is no reason here to add anything to explain it. And I have certainly the power of imagining likewise; for although it may happen (as I formerly supposed) that none of the things which I imagine are true, nevertheless this power of imagining does not cease to be really in use, and it forms part of my thought. Finally, I am the same who feels, that is to say, who perceives certain things, as by the organs of sense, since in truth I see light, I hear noise, I feel heat. But it will be said that these phenomena are false and that I am dreaming. Let it be so; still it is at least quite certain that it seems to me that I see light, that I hear noise and that I feel heat. That cannot be false; properly speaking it is what is in me called feeling[1]; and used in this precise sense that is no other thing than thinking.

From this time I begin to know what I am with a little more clearness and distinction than before; but nevertheless it still seems to me, and I cannot prevent myself from thinking, that corporeal things, whose images are framed by thought, which are tested by the senses, are much more distinctly known than that obscure part of me which does not come under the imagination. Although really it is very strange to say that I know and understand more distinctly these things whose existence seems to me

[1] Sentire.

dubious, which are unknown to me, and which do not belong to me, than others of the truth of which I am convinced, which are known to me and which pertain to my real nature, in a word, than myself. But I see clearly how the case stands : my mind loves to wander, and cannot yet suffer itself to be retained within the just limits of truth.   Very good, let us once more give it the freest rein, so that, when afterwards we seize the proper occasion for pulling up, it may the more easily be regulated and controlled.

Let us begin by considering the commonest matters, those which we believe to be the most distinctly comprehended, to wit, the bodies which we touch and see ; not indeed bodies in general, for these general ideas are usually a little more confused, but let us consider one body in particular.   Let us take, for example, this piece of wax : it has been taken quite freshly from the hive, and it has not yet lost the sweetness of the honey which it contains ; it still retains somewhat of the odour of the flowers from which it has been culled ; its colour, its figure, its size are apparent ; it is hard, cold, easily handled, and if you strike it with the finger, it will emit a sound. Finally all the things which are requisite to cause us distinctly to recognise a body, are met with in it.   But notice that while I speak and approach the fire what remained of the taste is exhaled, the smell evaporates, the colour alters, the figure is destroyed, the size increases, it becomes liquid, it heats, scarcely can one handle it, and when one strikes it, no sound is emitted.   Does the same wax remain after this change ?   We must confess that it remains ; none would judge otherwise.   What then did I know so distinctly in this piece of wax?   It could certainly be nothing of all that the senses brought to my notice, since all these things which fall under taste, smell, sight, touch, and hearing, are found to be changed, and yet the same wax remains.

Perhaps it was what I now think, viz. that this wax was not that sweetness of honey, nor that agreeable scent of flowers, nor that particular whiteness, nor that figure, nor that sound, but simply a body which a little while before appeared to me as perceptible under these forms, and which is now perceptible under others.   But what, precisely, is it that I imagine when I form such conceptions?   Let us attentively consider this, and, abstracting from all that does not belong to the wax, let us see what remains.   Certainly nothing remains excepting a certain extended thing which is flexible and movable.   But what is the meaning of flexible and movable ?   Is it not that I imagine that this piece of wax being round is capable of becoming square and of passing from a square to a triangular figure? No, certainly it is not that, since I imagine it admits of an infinitude of similar changes, and I nevertheless do not know how to compass the infinitude by my imagination, and consequently this conception which I have of the wax is not brought about by the faculty of imagination. What now is this extension? Is it not also unknown? For it becomes greater when the wax is melted, greater when it is boiled, and greater still when the heat increases; and I should not conceive [clearly] according to truth what wax is, if I did not think that even this piece that we are considering is capable of receiving more variations in extension than I have ever imagined. We must then grant that I could not even understand through the imagination what this piece of wax is, and that it is my mind[1] alone which perceives it. I say this piece of wax in particular, for as to wax in general it is yet clearer. But what is this piece of wax which cannot be understood excepting by the [understanding or] mind? It is certainly the same that I see, touch, imagine, and finally it is the same which I have always believed it to be from the beginning. But what must particularly be observed is that its perception is neither an act of vision, nor of touch, nor of imagination, and has never been such although it may have appeared formerly to be so, but only an intuition[2] of the mind, which may be imperfect and confused as it was formerly, or clear and distinct as it is at present, according as my attention is more or less directed to the elements which are found in it, and of which it is composed.

Yet in the meantime I am greatly astonished when I consider [the great feebleness of mind] and its proneness to fall [insensibly] into error; for although without giving expression to my thoughts I consider all this in my own mind, words often impede me and I am almost deceived by the terms of ordinary language. For we say that we see the same wax, if it is present, and not that we simply judge that it is the same from its having the same colour and figure. From this I should conclude that I knew the wax by means of vision and not simply by the intuition of the mind; unless by chance I remember that, when looking from a window and saying I see men who pass in the street, I really do not see them, but infer that what I see is men, just as I say that I see wax. And yet what do I see from the window but hats and coats which may cover automatic machines? Yet I judge these to be men. And similarly

---

[1] entendement F., mens L.   [2] inspectio.

solely by the faculty of judgment which rests in my mind, I comprehend that which I believed I saw with my eyes.

A man who makes it his aim to raise his knowledge above the common should be ashamed to derive the occasion for doubting from the forms of speech invented by the vulgar; I prefer to pass on and consider whether I had a more evident and perfect conception of what the wax was when I first perceived it, and when I believed I knew it by means of the external senses or at least by the common sense[1] as it is called, that is to say by the imaginative faculty, or whether my present conception is clearer now that I have most carefully examined what it is, and in what way it can be known. It would certainly be absurd to doubt as to this. For what was there in this first perception which was distinct? What was there which might not as well have been perceived by any of the animals? But when I distinguish the wax from its external forms, and when, just as if I had taken from it its vestments, I consider it quite naked, it is certain that although some error may still be found in my judgment, I can nevertheless not perceive it thus without a human mind.

But finally what shall I say of this mind, that is, of myself, for up to this point I do not admit in myself anything but mind? What then, I who seem to perceive this piece of wax so distinctly, do I not know myself, not only with much more truth and certainty, but also with much more distinctness and clearness? For if I judge that the wax is or exists from the fact that I see it, it certainly follows much more clearly that I am or that I exist myself from the fact that I see it. For it may be that what I see is not really wax, it may also be that I do not possess eyes with which to see anything; but it cannot be that when I see, or (for I no longer take account of the distinction) when I think I see, that I myself who think am nought. So if I judge that the wax exists from the fact that I touch it, the same thing will follow, to wit, that I am; and if I judge that my imagination, or some other cause, whatever it is, persuades me that the wax exists, I shall still conclude the same. And what I have here remarked of wax may be applied to all other things which are external to me [and which are met with outside of me]. And further, if the [notion or] perception of wax has seemed to me clearer and more distinct, not only after the sight or the touch, but also after many other causes have rendered it quite manifest to me, with how much more [evidence] and distinctness

---

[1] sensus communis.

must it be said that I now know myself, since all the reasons which contribute to the knowledge of wax, or any other body whatever, are yet better proofs of the nature of my mind! And there are so many other things in the mind itself which may contribute to the elucidation of its nature, that those which depend on body such as these just mentioned, hardly merit being taken into account.

But finally here I am, having insensibly reverted to the point I desired, for, since it is now manifest to me that even bodies are not properly speaking known by the senses or by the faculty of imagination, but by the understanding only, and since they are not known from the fact that they are seen or touched, but only because they are understood, I see clearly that there is nothing which is easier for me to know than my mind. But because it is difficult to rid oneself so promptly of an opinion to which one was accustomed for so long, it will be well that I should halt a little at this point, so that by the length of my meditation I may more deeply imprint on my memory this new knowledge.

MEDITATION III.

Of God: that He exists.

I shall now close my eyes, I shall stop my ears, I shall call away all my senses, I shall efface even from my thoughts all the images of corporeal things, or at least (for that is hardly possible) I shall esteem them as vain and false; and thus holding converse only with myself and considering my own nature, I shall try little by little to reach a better knowledge of and a more familiar acquaintanceship with myself. I am a thing that thinks, that is to say, that doubts, affirms, denies, that knows a few things, that is ignorant of many [that loves, that hates], that wills, that desires, that also imagines and perceives; for as I remarked before, although the things which I perceive and imagine are perhaps nothing at all apart from me and in themselves, I am nevertheless assured that these modes of thought that I call perceptions and imaginations, inasmuch only as they are modes of thought, certainly reside [and are met with] in me.

And in the little that I have just said, I think I have summed up all that I really know, or at least all that hitherto I was aware that I knew. In order to try to extend my knowledge further, I shall now look around more carefully and see whether I cannot still discover in myself some other things which I have not hitherto

perceived. I am certain that I am a thing which thinks; but do
I not then likewise know what is requisite to render me certain of
a truth? Certainly in this first knowledge there is nothing that
assures me of its truth, excepting the clear and distinct perception
of that which I state, which would not indeed suffice to assure me
that what I say is true, if it could ever happen that a thing which
I conceived so clearly and distinctly could be false; and accordingly
it seems to me that already I can establish as a general rule that
all things which I perceive[1] very clearly and very distinctly are true.

At the same time I have before received and admitted many
things to be very certain and manifest, which yet I afterwards
recognised as being dubious. What then were these things? They
were the earth, sky, stars and all other objects which I apprehended
by means of the senses. But what did I clearly [and distinctly]
perceive in them? Nothing more than that the ideas or thoughts
of these things were presented to my mind. And not even now
do I deny that these ideas are met with in me. But there was
yet another thing which I affirmed, and which, owing to the habit
which I had formed of believing it, I thought I perceived very
clearly, although in truth I did not perceive it at all, to wit, that
there were objects outside of me from which these ideas proceeded,
and to which they were entirely similar. And it was in this that
I erred, or, if perchance my judgment was correct, this was not due
to any knowledge arising from my perception.

But when I took anything very simple and easy in the sphere of
arithmetic or geometry into consideration, e.g. that two and three
together made five, and other things of the sort, were not these
present to my mind so clearly as to enable me to affirm that they
were true? Certainly if I judged that since such matters could be
doubted, this would not have been so for any other reason than that
it came into my mind that perhaps a God might have endowed
me with such a nature that I may have been deceived even
concerning things which seemed to me most manifest. But every
time that this preconceived opinion of the sovereign power of a God
presents itself to my thought, I am constrained to confess that it is
easy to Him, if He wishes it, to cause me to err, even in matters in
which I believe myself to have the best evidence. And, on the
other hand, always when I direct my attention to things which
I believe myself to perceive very clearly, I am so persuaded of their
truth that I let myself break out into words such as these: Let

---

[1] Percipio, F. *nous concevons.*

who will deceive me, He can never cause me to be nothing while
I think that I am, or some day cause it to be true to say that
I have never been, it being true now to say that I am, or that two
and three make more or less than five, or any such thing in which
I see a manifest contradiction. And, certainly, since I have no
reason to believe that there is a God who is a deceiver, and as
I have not yet satisfied myself that there is a God at all, the reason
for doubt which depends on this opinion alone is very slight, and so
to speak metaphysical. But in order to be able altogether to
remove it, I must inquire whether there is a God as soon as the
occasion presents itself; and if I find that there is a God, I must
also inquire whether He may be a deceiver; for without a knowledge
of these two truths I do not see that I can ever be certain of
anything.

And in order that I may have an opportunity of inquiring into
this in an orderly way [without interrupting the order of meditation
which I have proposed to myself, and which is little by little to
pass from the notions which I find first of all in my mind to those
which I shall later on discover in it] it is requisite that I should
here divide my thoughts into certain kinds, and that I should
consider in which of these kinds there is, properly speaking, truth
or error to be found. Of my thoughts some are, so to speak, images
of the things, and to these alone is the title 'idea' properly applied;
examples are my thought of a man or of a chimera, of heaven, of
an angel, or [even] of God. But other thoughts possess other
forms as well. For example in willing, fearing, approving, denying,
though I always perceive something as the subject of the action
of my mind[1], yet by this action I always add something else to the
idea[2] which I have of that thing; and of the thoughts of this kind
some are called volitions or affections, and others judgments.

Now as to what concerns ideas, if we consider them only in
themselves and do not relate them to anything else beyond
themselves, they cannot properly speaking be false; for whether
I imagine a goat or a chimera, it is not less true that I imagine the
one than the other. We must no fear likewise that falsity can
enter into will and into affections, for although I may desire evil
things, or even things that never existed, it is not the less true that
I desire them. Thus there remains no more than the judgments

(margin handwritten note: mistaken that it could exist)

---

[1] The French version is followed here as being more explicit. In it 'action
de mon esprit' replaces 'mea cogitatio.'
[2] In the Latin version 'similitudinem.'

which we make, in which I must take the greatest care not to
deceive myself.   But the principal error and the commonest which
we may meet with in them, consists in my judging that the ideas
which are in me are similar or conformable to the things which are
outside me; for without doubt if I considered the ideas only as
certain modes of my thoughts, without trying to relate them to
anything beyond, they could scarcely give me material for error.

But among these ideas, some appear to me to be innate, some
adventitious, and others to be formed [or invented] by myself; for,
as I have the power of understanding what is called a thing, or a
truth, or a thought, it appears to me that I hold this power from
no other source than my own nature.   But if I now hear some sound,
if I see the sun, or feel heat, I have hitherto judged that these
sensations proceeded from certain things that exist outside of me;
and finally it appears to me that sirens, hippogryphs, and the like,
are formed out of my own mind.   But again I may possibly
persuade myself that all these ideas are of the nature of those which
I term adventitious, or else that they are all innate, or all fictitious:
for I have not yet clearly discovered their true origin.

And my principal task in this place is to consider, in respect to
those ideas which appear to me to proceed from certain objects that
are outside me, what are the reasons which cause me to think them
similar to these objects.   It seems indeed in the first place that
I am taught this lesson by nature ; and, secondly, I experience in
myself that these ideas do not depend on my will nor therefore on
myself—for they often present themselves to my mind in spite of
my will.   Just now, for instance, whether I will or whether I do not
will, I feel heat, and thus I persuade myself that this feeling, or at
least this idea of heat, is produced in me by something which is
different from me, i.e. by the heat of the fire near which I sit.
And nothing seems to me more obvious than to judge that this
object imprints its likeness rather than anything else upon me.

Now I must discover whether these proofs are sufficiently strong
and convincing.   When I say that I am so instructed by nature,
I merely mean a certain spontaneous inclination which impels me
to believe in this connection, and not a natural light which makes
me recognise that it is true.   But these two things are very
different ; for I cannot doubt that which the natural light causes
me to believe to be true, as, for example, it has shown me that I am
from the fact that I doubt, or other facts of the same kind.   And
I possess no other faculty whereby to distinguish truth from false-

hood, which can teach me that what this light shows me to be true
is not really true, and no other faculty that is equally trustworthy.
But as far as [apparently] natural impulses are concerned, I have
frequently remarked, when I had to make active choice between
virtue and vice, that they often enough led me to the part that was
worse; and this is why I do not see any reason for following them
in what regards truth and error.

And as to the other reason, which is that these ideas must
proceed from objects outside me, since they do not depend on
my will, I do not find it any the more convincing. For just as
these impulses of which I have spoken are found in me, notwithstanding that they do not always concur with my will, so perhaps
there is in me some faculty fitted to produce these ideas without
the assistance of any external things, even though it is not yet
known by me; just as, apparently, they have hitherto always been
found in me during sleep without the aid of any external objects.

And finally, though they did proceed from objects different
from myself, it is not a necessary consequence that they should
resemble these. On the contrary, I have noticed that in many
cases there was a great difference between the object and its idea.
I find, for example, two completely diverse ideas of the sun in my
mind; the one derives its origin from the senses, and should be
placed in the category of adventitious ideas; according to this
idea the sun seems to be extremely small; but the other is derived
from astronomical reasonings, i.e. is elicited from certain notions
that are innate in me, or else it is formed by me in some other
manner; in accordance with it the sun appears to be several times
greater than the earth. These two ideas cannot, indeed, both
resemble the same sun, and reason makes me believe that the one
which seems to have originated directly from the sun itself, is the
one which is most dissimilar to it.

All this causes me to believe that until the present time it has
not been by a judgment that was certain [or premeditated], but
only by a sort of blind impulse that I believed that things existed
outside of, and different from me, which, by the organs of my
senses, or by some other method whatever it might be, conveyed
these ideas or images to me [and imprinted on me their
similitudes].

But there is yet another method of inquiring whether any of
the objects of which I have ideas within me exist outside of me
If ideas are only taken as certain modes of thought, I recognise

amongst them no difference or inequality, and all appear to proceed
from me in the same manner; but when we consider them as
images, one representing one thing and the other another, it is clear
that they are very different one from the other. There is no doubt
that those which represent to me substances are something more,
and contain so to speak more objective reality within them [that is
to say, by representation participate in a higher degree of being or
perfection] than those that simply represent modes or accidents ;
and that idea again by which I understand a supreme God, eternal,
infinite, [immutable], omniscient, omnipotent, and Creator of all
things which are outside of Himself, has certainly more objective
reality in itself than those ideas by which finite substances are
represented.

Now it is manifest by the natural light that there must at least
be as much reality in the efficient and total cause as in its effect.
For, pray, whence can the effect derive its reality, if not from its
cause? And in what way can this cause communicate this reality
to it, unless it possessed it in itself? And from this it follows, not
only that something cannot proceed from nothing, but likewise
that what is more perfect—that is to say, which has more reality
within itself—cannot proceed from the less perfect. And this is
not only evidently true of those effects which possess actual or
formal reality, but also of the ideas in which we consider merely
what is termed objective reality. To take an example, the stone
which has not yet existed not only cannot now commence to be
unless it has been produced by something which possesses within
itself, either formally or eminently, all that enters into the
composition of the stone [i.e. it must possess the same things or
other more excellent things than those which exist in the stone]
and heat can only be produced in a subject in which it did not
previously exist by a cause that is of an order [degree or kind] at
least as perfect as heat, and so in all other cases. But further,
the idea of heat, or of a stone, cannot exist in me unless it has
been placed within me by some cause which possesses within it at
least as much reality as that which I conceive to exist in the heat
or the stone. For although this cause does not transmit anything
of its actual or formal reality to my idea, we must not for that
reason imagine that it is necessarily a less real cause ; we must
remember that [since every idea is a work of the mind] its nature
is such that it demands of itself no other formal reality than that
which it borrows from my thought, of which it is only a mode

[i.e. a manner or way of thinking]. But in order that an idea should contain some one certain objective reality rather than another, it must without doubt derive it from some cause in which there is at least as much formal reality as this idea contains of objective reality. For if we imagine that something is found in an idea which is not found in the cause, it must then have been derived from nought; but however imperfect may be this mode of being by which a thing is objectively [or by representation] in the understanding by its idea, we cannot certainly say that this mode of being is nothing, nor, consequently, that the idea derives its origin from nothing.

Nor must I imagine that, since the reality that I consider in these ideas is only objective, it is not essential that this reality should be formally in the causes of my ideas, but that it is sufficient that it should be found objectively. For just as this mode of objective existence pertains to ideas by their proper nature, so does the mode of formal existence pertain to the causes of those ideas (this is at least true of the first and principal) by the nature peculiar to them. And although it may be the case that one idea gives birth to another idea, that cannot continue to be so indefinitely; for in the end we must reach an idea whose cause shall be so to speak an archetype, in which the whole reality [or perfection] which is so to speak objectively [or by representation] in these ideas is contained formally [and really]. Thus the light of nature causes me to know clearly that the ideas in me are like [pictures or] images which can, in truth, easily fall short of the perfection of the objects from which they have been derived, but which can never contain anything greater or more perfect.

And the longer and the more carefully that I investigate these matters, the more clearly and distinctly do I recognise their truth. But what am I to conclude from it all in the end? It is this, that if the objective reality of any one of my ideas is of such a nature as clearly to make me recognise that it is not in me either formally or eminently, and that consequently I cannot myself be the cause of it, it follows of necessity that I am not alone in the world, but that there is another being which exists, or which is the cause of this idea. On the other hand, had no such an idea existed in me, I should have had no sufficient argument to convince me of the existence of any being beyond myself; for I have made very careful investigation everywhere and up to the present time have been able to find no other ground.

But of my ideas, beyond that which represents me to myself, as to which there can here be no difficulty, there is another which represents a God, and there are others representing corporeal and inanimate things, others angels, others animals, and others again which represent to me men similar to myself.

As regards the ideas which represent to me other men or animals, or angels, I can however easily conceive that they might be formed by an admixture of the other ideas which I have of myself, of corporeal things, and of God, even although there were apart from me neither men nor animals, nor angels, in all the world.

And in regard to the ideas of corporeal objects, I do not recognise in them anything so great or so excellent that they might not have possibly proceeded from myself; for if I consider them more closely, and examine them individually, as I yesterday examined the idea of wax, I find that there is very little in them which I perceive clearly and distinctly. Magnitude or extension in length, breadth, or depth, I do so perceive; also figure which results from a termination of this extension, the situation which bodies of different figure preserve in relation to one another, and movement or change of situation; to which we may also add substance, duration and number. As to other things such as light, colours, sounds, scents, tastes, heat, cold and the other tactile qualities, they are thought by me with so much obscurity and confusion that I do not even know if they are true or false, i.e. whether the ideas which I form of these qualities are actually the ideas of real objects or not [or whether they only represent chimeras which cannot exist in fact]. For although I have before remarked that it is only in judgments that falsity, properly speaking, or formal falsity, can be met with, a certain material falsity may nevertheless be found in ideas, i.e. when these ideas represent what is nothing as though it were something. For example, the ideas which I have of cold and heat are so far from clear and distinct that by their means I cannot tell whether cold is merely a privation of heat, or heat a privation of cold, or whether both are real qualities, or are not such. And inasmuch as [since ideas resemble images] there cannot be any ideas which do not appear to represent some things, if it is correct to say that cold is merely a privation of heat, the idea which represents it to me as something real and positive will not be improperly termed false, and the same holds good of other similar ideas.

To these it is certainly not necessary that I should attribute any author other than myself. For if they are false, i.e. if they represent things which do not exist, the light of nature shows me that they issue from nought, that is to say, that they are only in me in so far as something is lacking to the perfection of my nature. But if they are true, nevertheless because they exhibit so little reality to me that I cannot even clearly distinguish the thing represented from non-being, I do not see any reason why they should not be produced by myself.

As to the clear and distinct idea which I have of corporeal things, some of them seem as though I might have derived them from the idea which I possess of myself, as those which I have of substance, duration, number, and such like. For [even] when I think that a stone is a substance, or at least a thing capable of existing of itself, and that I am a substance also, although I conceive that I am a thing that thinks and not one that is extended, and that the stone on the other hand is an extended thing which does not think, and that thus there is a notable difference between the two conceptions—they seem, nevertheless, to agree in this, that both represent substances. In the same way, when I perceive that I now exist and further recollect that I have in former times existed, and when I remember that I have various thoughts of which I can recognise the number, I acquire ideas of duration and number which I can afterwards transfer to any object that I please. But as to all the other qualities of which the ideas of corporeal things are composed, to wit, extension, figure, situation and motion, it is true that they are not formally in me, since I am only a thing that thinks; but because they are merely certain modes of substance [and so to speak the vestments under which corporeal substance appears to us] and because I myself am also a substance, it would seem that they might be contained in me eminently.

Hence there remains only the idea of God, concerning which we must consider whether it is something which cannot have proceeded from me myself. By the name God I understand a substance that is infinite [eternal, immutable], independent, all-knowing, all-powerful, and by which I myself and everything else, if anything else does exist, have been created. Now all these characteristics are such that the more diligently I attend to them, the less do they appear capable of proceeding from me alone; hence, from what has been already said, we must conclude that God necessarily exists.

[handwritten margin, left, vertical] omnipresent, omniscent, omnipotent, omnibenevolent, perfect, kind, power

[handwritten margin, right, vertical] qualities that exist like in deus

[handwritten note, bottom] God is the necessary being because of the nature of god eternal, immutable, infinity

For although the idea of substance is within me owing to the fact that I am substance, nevertheless I should not have the idea of an infinite substance—since I am finite—if it had not proceeded from some substance which was veritably infinite.

Nor should I imagine that I do not perceive the infinite by a true idea, but only by the negation of the finite, just as I perceive repose and darkness by the negation of movement and of light; for, on the contrary, I see that there is manifestly more reality in infinite substance than in finite, and therefore that in some way I have in me the notion of the infinite earlier than the finite—to wit, the notion of God before that of myself. For how would it be possible that I should know that I doubt and desire, that is to say, that something is lacking to me, and that I am not quite perfect, unless I had within me some idea of a Being more perfect than myself, in comparison with which I should recognise the deficiencies of my nature?

And we cannot say that this idea of God is perhaps materially false and that consequently I can derive it from nought [i.e. that possibly it exists in me because I am imperfect], as I have just said is the case with ideas of heat, cold and other such things; for, on the contrary, as this idea is very clear and distinct and contains within it more objective reality than any other, there can be none which is of itself more true, nor any in which there can be less suspicion of falsehood. The idea, I say, of this Being who is absolutely perfect and infinite, is entirely true; for although, perhaps, we can imagine that such a Being does not exist, we cannot nevertheless imagine that His idea represents nothing real to me, as I have said of the idea of cold. This idea is also very clear and distinct; since all that I conceive clearly and distinctly of the real and the true, and of what conveys some perfection, is in its entirety contained in this idea. And this does not cease to be true although I do not comprehend the infinite, or though in God there is an infinitude of things which I cannot comprehend, nor possibly even reach in any way by thought; for it is of the nature of the infinite that my nature, which is finite and limited, should not comprehend it; and it is sufficient that I should understand this, and that I should judge that all things which I clearly perceive and in which I know that there is some perfection, and possibly likewise an infinitude of properties of which I am ignorant, are in God formally or eminently, so that the idea which I have of Him may become the most true, most clear, and most distinct of all the ideas that are in my mind.

But possibly I am something more than I suppose myself to be, and perhaps all those perfections which I attribute to God are in some way potentially in me, although they do not yet disclose themselves, or issue in action. As a matter of fact I am already sensible that my knowledge increases [and perfects itself] little by little, and I see nothing which can prevent it from increasing more and more into infinitude; nor do I see, after it has thus been increased [or perfected], anything to prevent my being able to acquire by its means all the other perfections of the Divine nature; nor finally why the power I have of acquiring these perfections, if it really exists in me, shall not suffice to produce the ideas of them.

At the same time I recognise that this cannot be. For, in the first place, although it were true that every day my knowledge acquired new degrees of perfection, and that there were in my nature many things potentially which are not yet there actually, nevertheless these excellences do not pertain to [or make the smallest approach to] the idea which I have of God in whom there is nothing merely potential [but in whom all is present really and actually]; for it is an infallible token of imperfection in my knowledge that it increases little by little. And further, although my knowledge grows more and more, nevertheless I do not for that reason believe that it can ever be actually infinite, since it can never reach a point so high that it will be unable to attain to any greater increase. But I understand God to be actually infinite, so that He can add nothing to His supreme perfection. And finally I perceive that the objective being of an idea cannot be produced by a being that exists potentially only, which properly speaking is nothing, but only by a being which is formal or actual.

To speak the truth, I see nothing in all that I have just said which by the light of nature is not manifest to anyone who desires to think attentively on the subject; but when I slightly relax my attention, my mind, finding its vision somewhat obscured and so to speak blinded by the images of sensible objects, I do not easily re-collect the reason why the idea that I possess of a being more perfect than I, must necessarily have been placed in me by a being which is really more perfect; and this is why I wish here to go on to inquire whether I, who have this idea, can exist if no such being exists.

And I ask, from whom do I then derive my existence? Perhaps from myself or from my parents, or from some other source less perfect than God; for we can imagine nothing more perfect than God, or even as perfect as He is.

But [were I independent of every other and] were I myself the author of my being, I should doubt nothing and I should desire nothing, and finally no perfection would be lacking to me; for I should have bestowed on myself every perfection of which I possessed any idea and should thus be God. And it must not be imagined that those things that are lacking to me are perhaps more difficult of attainment than those which I already possess; for, on the contrary, it is quite evident that it was a matter of much greater difficulty to bring to pass that I, that is to say, a thing or a substance that thinks, should emerge out of nothing, than it would be to attain to the knowledge of many things of which I am ignorant, and which are only the accidents of this thinking substance. But it is clear that if I had of myself possessed this greater perfection of which I have just spoken [that is to say, if I had been the author of my own existence], I should not at least have denied myself the things which are the more easy to acquire [to wit, many branches of knowledge of which my nature is destitute]; nor should I have deprived myself of any of the things contained in the idea which I form of God, because there are none of them which seem to me specially difficult to acquire: and if there were any that were more difficult to acquire, they would certainly appear to me to be such (supposing I myself were the origin of the other things which I possess) since I should discover in them that my powers were limited.

But though I assume that perhaps I have always existed just as I am at present, neither can I escape the force of this reasoning, and imagine that the conclusion to be drawn from this is, that I need not seek for any author of my existence. For all the course of my life may be divided into an infinite number of parts, none of which is in any way dependent on the other; and thus from the fact that I was in existence a short time ago it does not follow that I must be in existence now, unless some cause at this instant, so to speak, produces me anew, that is to say, conserves me. It is as a matter of fact perfectly clear and evident to all those who consider with attention the nature of time, that, in order to be conserved in each moment in which it endures, a substance has need of the same power and action as would be necessary to produce and create it anew, supposing it did not yet exist, so that the light of nature shows us clearly that the distinction between creation and conservation is solely a distinction of the reason.

All that I thus require here is that I should interrogate myself, if I wish to know whether I possess a power which is capable of bringing it to pass that I who now am shall still be in the future; for since I am nothing but a thinking thing, or at least since thus far it is only this portion of myself which is precisely in question at present, if such a power did reside in me, I should certainly be conscious of it. But I am conscious of nothing of the kind, and by this I know clearly that I depend on some being different from myself.

Possibly, however, this being on which I depend is not that which I call God, and I am created either by my parents or by some other cause less perfect than God. This cannot be, because, as I have just said, it is perfectly evident that there must be at least as much reality in the cause as in the effect; and thus since I am a thinking thing, and possess an idea of God within me, whatever in the end be the cause assigned to my existence, it must be allowed that it is likewise a thinking thing and that it possesses in itself the idea of all the perfections which I attribute to God. We may again inquire whether this cause derives its origin from itself or from some other thing. For if from itself, it follows by the reasons before brought forward, that this cause must itself be God; for since it possesses the virtue of self-existence, it must also without doubt have the power of actually possessing all the perfections of which it has the idea, that is, all those which I conceive as existing in God. But if it derives its existence from some other cause than itself, we shall again ask, for the same reason, whether this second cause exists by itself or through another, until from one step to another, we finally arrive at an ultimate cause, which will be God.

And it is perfectly manifest that in this there can be no regression into infinity, since what is in question is not so much the cause which formerly created me, as that which conserves me at the present time.

Nor can we suppose that several causes may have concurred in my production, and that from one I have received the idea of one of the perfections which I attribute to God, and from another the idea of some other, so that all these perfections indeed exist somewhere in the universe, but not as complete in one unity which is God. On the contrary, the unity, the simplicity or the inseparability of all things which are in God is one of the principal perfections which I conceive to be in Him. And certainly the idea of this unity of all Divine perfections cannot have been placed in me by any cause from which I have not likewise received the ideas of all the other perfections; for this cause could not make me able to comprehend them as joined together in an inseparable unity without having at the same time caused me in some measure to know what they are [and in some way to recognise each one of them].

Finally, so far as my parents [from whom it appears I have sprung] are concerned, although all that I have ever been able to believe of them were true, that does not make it follow that it is they who conserve me, nor are they even the authors of my being in any sense, in so far as I am a thinking being; since what they did was merely to implant certain dispositions in that matter in which the self—i.e. the mind, which alone I at present identify with myself—is by me deemed to exist. And thus there can be no difficulty in their regard, but we must of necessity conclude from the fact alone that I exist, or that the idea of a Being supremely perfect—that is of God—is in me, that the proof of God's existence is grounded on the highest evidence.

It only remains to me to examine into the manner in which I have acquired this idea from God; for I have not received it through the senses, and it is never presented to me unexpectedly, as is usual with the ideas of sensible things when these things present themselves, or seem to present themselves, to the external organs of my senses; nor is it likewise a fiction of my mind, for it is not in my power to take from or to add anything to it; and consequently the only alternative is that it is innate in me, just as the idea of myself is innate in me.

And one certainly ought not to find it strange that God, in creating me, placed this idea within me to be like the mark of the workman imprinted on his work; and it is likewise not essential that the mark shall be something different from the work itself. For from the sole fact that God created me it is most probable that in some way he has placed his image and similitude upon me, and that I perceive this similitude (in which the idea of God is contained) by means of the same faculty by which I perceive myself—that is to say, when I reflect on myself I not only know that I am something [imperfect], incomplete and dependent on another, which incessantly aspires after something which is better and greater than myself, but I also know that He on whom I depend possesses in Himself all the great things towards which I aspire [and the ideas of which I find within myself], and that not indefinitely or potentially alone, but really, actually and infinitely; and that thus He is God. And the whole strength of the argument which I have here made use of to prove the existence of God consists in this, that I recognise that it is not possible that my nature should be what it is, and indeed that I should have in myself the idea of a God, if God did not veritably exist—a God, I say, whose idea is in me, i.e. who possesses all those supreme perfections of which our mind may indeed have some idea but without understanding them all, who is liable to no errors or defect [and who has none of all those marks which denote imperfection]. From this it is manifest that He cannot be a deceiver, since the light of nature teaches us that fraud and deception necessarily proceed from some defect.

But before I examine this matter with more care, and pass on to the consideration of other truths which may be derived from it, it seems to me right to pause for a while in order to contemplate God Himself, to ponder at leisure His marvellous attributes, to consider, and admire, and adore, the beauty of this light so resplendent, at least as far as the strength of my mind, which is in some measure dazzled by the sight, will allow me to do so. For just as faith teaches us that the supreme felicity of the other life consists only in this contemplation of the Divine Majesty, so we continue to learn by experience that a similar meditation, though incomparably less perfect, causes us to enjoy the greatest satisfaction of which we are capable in this life.

MEDITATION IV.

Of the True and the False.

I have been well accustomed these past days to detach my mind from my senses, and I have accurately observed that there are very few things that one knows with certainty respecting corporeal objects, that there are many more which are known to us respecting the human mind, and yet more still regarding God Himself ; so that I shall now without any difficulty abstract my thoughts from the consideration of [sensible or] imaginable objects, and carry them to those which, being withdrawn from all contact with matter, are purely intelligible. And certainly the idea which I possess of the human mind inasmuch as it is a thinking thing, and not extended in length, width and depth, nor participating in anything pertaining to body, is incomparably more distinct than is the idea of any corporeal thing. And when I consider that I doubt, that is to say, that I am an incomplete and dependent being, the idea of a being that is complete and independent, that is of God, presents itself to my mind with so much distinctness and clearness—and from the fact alone that this idea is found in me, or that I who possess this idea exist, I conclude so certainly that God exists, and that my existence depends entirely on Him in every moment of my life— that I do not think that the human mind is capable of knowing anything with more evidence and certitude. And it seems to me that I now have before me a road which will lead us from the contemplation of the true God (in whom all the treasures of science and wisdom are contained) to the knowledge of the other objects of the universe.

For, first of all, I recognise it to be impossible that He should ever deceive me ; for in all fraud and deception some imperfection is to be found, and although it may appear that the power of deception is a mark of subtilty or power, yet the desire to deceive without doubt testifies to malice or feebleness, and accordingly cannot be found in God.

In the next place I experienced in myself a certain capacity for judging which I have doubtless received from God, like all the other things that I possess ; and as He could not desire to deceive me, it is clear that He has not given me a faculty that will lead me to err if I use it aright.

And no doubt respecting this matter could remain, if it were not that the consequence would seem to follow that I can thus never be deceived ; for if I hold all that I possess from God, and if He has not placed in me the capacity for error, it seems as though I could never fall into error. And it is true that when I think only of God [and direct my mind wholly to Him]¹, I discover [in myself] no cause of error, or falsity; yet directly afterwards, when recurring to myself, experience shows me that I am nevertheless subject to an infinitude of errors, as to which, when we come to investigate them more closely, I notice that not only is there a real and positive idea of God or of a Being of supreme perfection present to my mind, but also, so to speak, a certain negative idea of nothing, that is, of that which is infinitely removed from any kind of perfection; and that I am in a sense something intermediate between God and nought, i.e. placed in such a manner between the supreme Being and non-being, that there is in truth nothing in me that can lead to error in so far as a sovereign Being has formed me ; but that, as I in some degree participate likewise in nought or in non-being, i.e. in so far as I am not myself the supreme Being, and as I find myself subject

¹ Not in the French version.

to an infinitude of imperfections, I ought not to be astonished if I should fall into error. Thus do I recognise that error, in so far as it is such, is not a real thing depending on God, but simply a defect; and therefore, in order to fall into it, that I have no need to possess a special faculty given me by God for this very purpose, but that I fall into error from the fact that the power given me by God for the purpose of distinguishing truth from error is not infinite.

Nevertheless this does not quite satisfy me; for error is not a pure negation [i.e. is not the simple defect or want of some perfection which ought not to be mine], but it is a lack of some knowledge which it seems that I ought to possess. And on considering the nature of God it does not appear to me possible that He should have given me a faculty which is not perfect of its kind, that is, which is wanting in some perfection due to it. For if it is true that the more skilful the artizan, the more perfect is the work of his hands, what can have been produced by this supreme Creator of all things that is not in all its parts perfect? And certainly there is no doubt that God could have created me so that I could never have been subject to error; it is also certain that He ever wills what is best; is it then better that I should be subject to err than that I should not?

In considering this more attentively, it occurs to me in the first place that I should not be astonished if my intelligence is not capable of comprehending why God acts as He does; and that there is thus no reason to doubt of His existence from the fact that I may perhaps find many other things besides this as to which I am able to understand neither for what reason nor how God has produced them. For, in the first place, knowing that my nature is extremely feeble and limited, and that the nature of God is on the contrary immense, incomprehensible, and infinite, I have no further difficulty in recognising that there is an infinitude of matters in His power, the causes of which transcend my knowledge; and this reason suffices to convince me that the species of cause termed final, finds no useful employment in physical [or natural] things; for it does not appear to me that I can without temerity seek to investigate the [inscrutable] ends of God.

It further occurs to me that we should not consider one single creature separately, when we inquire as to whether the works of God are perfect, but should regard all his creations together. For the same thing which might possibly seem very imperfect with some

Part of something bigger

semblance of reason if regarded by itself, is found to be very perfect if regarded as part of the whole universe; and although, since I resolved to doubt all things, I as yet have only known certainly my own existence and that of God, nevertheless since I have recognised the infinite power of God, I cannot deny that He may have produced many other things, or at least that He has the power of producing them, so that I may obtain a place as a part of a great universe.

Whereupon, regarding myself more closely, and considering what are my errors (for they alone testify to there being any imperfection in me), I answer that they depend on a combination of two causes, to wit, on the faculty of knowledge that rests in me, and on the power of choice or of free will—that is to say, of the understanding and at the same time of the will. For by the understanding alone I [neither assert nor deny anything, but] apprehend[1] the ideas of things as to which I can form a judgment. But no error is properly speaking found in it, provided the word error is taken in its proper signification; and though there is possibly an infinitude of things in the world of which I have no idea in my understanding, we cannot for all that say that it is deprived of these ideas [as we might say of something which is required by its nature], but simply it does not possess these; because in truth there is no reason to prove that God should have given me a greater faculty of knowledge than He has given me; and however skilful a workman I represent Him to be, I should not for all that consider that He was bound to have placed in each of His works all the perfections which He may have been able to place in some. I likewise cannot complain that God has not given me a free choice or a will which is sufficient, ample and perfect, since as a matter of fact I am conscious of a will so extended as to be subject to no limits. And what seems to me very remarkable in this regard is that of all the qualities which I possess there is no one so perfect and so comprehensive that I do not very clearly recognise that it might be yet greater and more perfect. For, to take an example, if I consider the faculty of comprehension which I possess, I find that it is of very small extent and extremely limited, and at the same time I find the idea of another faculty much more ample and even infinite, and seeing that I can form the idea of it, I recognise from this very fact that it pertains to the nature of God. If in the same way I examine the memory, the imagination, or some other faculty, I do not find any which is not

[1] percipio.

small and circumscribed, while in God it is immense [or infinite]. It is free-will alone or liberty of choice which I find to be so great in me that I can conceive no other idea to be more great; it is indeed the case that it is for the most part this will that causes me to know that in some manner I bear the image and similitude of God. For although the power of will is incomparably greater in God than in me, both by reason of the knowledge and the power which, conjoined with it, render it stronger and more efficacious, and by reason of its object, inasmuch as in God it extends to a great many things; it nevertheless does not seem to me greater if I consider it formally and precisely in itself: for the faculty of will consists alone in our having the power of choosing to do a thing or choosing not to do it (that is, to affirm or deny, to pursue or to shun it), or rather it consists alone in the fact that in order to affirm or deny, pursue or shun those things placed before us by the understanding, we act so that we are unconscious that any outside force constrains us in doing so. For in order that I should be free it is not necessary that I should be indifferent as to the choice of one or the other of two contraries; but contrariwise the more I lean to the one—whether I recognise clearly that the reasons of the good and true are to be found in it, or whether God so disposes my inward thought—the more freely do I choose and embrace it. And undoubtedly both divine grace and natural knowledge, far from diminishing my liberty, rather increase it and strengthen it. Hence this indifference which I feel, when I am not swayed to one side rather than to the other by lack of reason, is the lowest grade of liberty, and rather evinces a lack or negation in knowledge than a perfection of will: for if I always recognised clearly what was true and good, I should never have trouble in deliberating as to what judgment or choice I should make, and then I should be entirely free without ever being indifferent.

From all this I recognise that the power of will which I have received from God is not of itself the source of my errors—for it is very ample and very perfect of its kind—any more than is the power of understanding; for since I understand nothing but by the power which God has given me for understanding, there is no doubt that all that I understand, I understand as I ought, and it is not possible that I err in this. Whence then come my errors? They come from the sole fact that since the will is much wider in its range and compass than the understanding, I do not restrain it within the same bounds, but extend it also to things which I do not understand: and as the will is of itself indifferent to these, it easily falls into error and sin, and chooses the evil for the good, or the false for the true.

For example, when I lately examined whether anything existed in the world, and found that from the very fact that I considered this question it followed very clearly that I myself existed, I could not prevent myself from believing that a thing I so clearly conceived was true: not that I found myself compelled to do so by some external cause, but simply because from great clearness in my mind there followed a great inclination of my will; and I believed this with so much the greater freedom or spontaneity as I possessed the less indifference towards it. Now, on the contrary, I not only know that I exist, inasmuch as I am a thinking thing, but a certain representation of corporeal nature is also presented to my mind; and it comes to pass that I doubt whether this thinking nature which is in me, or rather by which I am what I am, differs from this corporeal nature, or whether both are not simply the same thing; and I here suppose that I do not yet know any reason to persuade me to adopt the one belief rather than the other. From this it follows that I am entirely indifferent as to which of the two I affirm or deny, or even whether I abstain from forming any judgment in the matter.

And this indifference does not only extend to matters as to which the understanding has no knowledge, but also in general to all those which are not apprehended with perfect clearness at the moment when the will is deliberating upon them: for, however probable are the conjectures which render me disposed to form a judgment respecting anything, the simple knowledge that I have that those are conjectures alone and not certain and indubitable reasons, suffices to occasion me to judge the contrary. Of this I have had great experience of late when I set aside as false all that I had formerly held to be absolutely true, for the sole reason that I remarked that it might in some measure be doubted.

But if I abstain from giving my judgment on any thing when I do not perceive it with sufficient clearness and distinctness, it is plain that I act rightly and am not deceived. But if I determine to deny or affirm, I no longer make use as I should of my free will, and if I affirm what is not true, it is evident that I deceive myself; even though I judge according to truth, this comes about only by chance, and I do not escape the blame of misusing my freedom; for the light of nature teaches us that the knowledge of the understanding should always precede the determination of the will.

And it is in the misuse of the free will that the privation which constitutes the characteristic nature of error is met with. Privation, I say, is found in the act, in so far as it proceeds from me, but it is not found in the faculty which I have received from God, nor even in the act in so far as it depends on Him.

For I have certainly no cause to complain that God has not given me an intelligence which is more powerful, or a natural light which is stronger than that which I have received from Him, since it is proper to the finite understanding not to comprehend a multitude of things, and it is proper to a created understanding to be finite ; on the contrary, I have every reason to render thanks to God who owes me nothing and who has given me all the perfections I possess, and I should be far from charging Him with injustice, and with having deprived me of, or wrongfully withheld from me, these perfections which He has not bestowed upon me.

I have further no reason to complain that He has given me a will more ample than my understanding, for since the will consists only of one single element, and is so to speak indivisible, it appears that its nature is such that nothing can be abstracted from it [without destroying it]; and certainly the more comprehensive it is found to be, the more reason I have to render gratitude to the giver.

And, finally, I must also not complain that God concurs with me in forming the acts of the will, that is the judgment in which I go astray, because these acts are entirely true and good, inasmuch as they depend on God; and in a certain sense more perfection accrues to my nature from the fact that I can form them, than if I could not do so. As to the privation in which alone the formal reason of error or sin consists, it has no need of any concurrence from God, since it is not a thing [or an existence], and since it is not related to God as to a cause, but should be termed merely a negation [according to the significance given to these words in the Schools]. For in fact it is not an imperfection in God that He has given me the liberty to give or withhold my assent from certain things as to which He has not placed a clear and distinct knowledge in my understanding ; but it is without doubt an imperfection in me not to make a good use of my freedom, and to give my judgment readily on matters which I only understand obscurely. I neverthe- less perceive that God could easily have created me so that I never should err, although I still remained free, and endowed with a limited knowledge, viz. by giving to my understanding a clear and distinct intelligence of all things as to which I should ever have to deliberate ; or simply by His engraving deeply in my memory the resolution never to form a judgment on anything without having a clear and distinct understanding of it, so that I could never forget it. And it is easy for me to understand that, in so far as I consider myself alone, and as if there were only myself in the world, I should have been much more perfect than I am, if God had created me so that I could never err. Nevertheless I cannot deny that in some sense it is a greater perfection in the whole universe that certain parts should not be exempt from error as others are than that all parts should be exactly similar. And I have no right to·complain if God, having placed me in .the world, has not called upon me to play a part that excels all others in distinction and perfection.

And further I have reason to be glad on the ground that if He has not given me the power of never going astray by the first means pointed out above, which depends on a clear and evident knowledge of all the things regarding which I can deliberate, He has at least left within my power the other means, which is firmly to adhere to the resolution never to give judgment on matters whose truth is not clearly known to me ; for although I notice a certain weakness in my nature in that I cannot continually concentrate my mind on one single thought, I can yet, by attentive and frequently repeated meditation, impress it so forcibly on my memory that I shall never fail to recollect it whenever I have need of it, and thus acquire the habit of never going astray.

And inasmuch as it is in this that the greatest and principal perfection of man consists, it seems to me that I have not gained little by this day's Meditation, since I have discovered the source of falsity and error. And certainly there can be no other source than that which I have explained ; for as often as I so restrain my will within the limits of my knowledge that it forms no judgment except on matters which are clearly and distinctly represented to it by the understanding, I can never be deceived; for every clear and distinct conception[1] is without doubt something, and hence cannot derive its origin from what is nought, but must of necessity have God as its author—God, I say, who being supremely perfect, cannot be the cause of any error ; and consequently we must conclude that such a conception [or such a judgment] is true. Nor have I only learned to-day what I should avoid in order that I may not err, but also how I should act in order to arrive at a knowledge of the

---

[1] perceptio.

truth; for without doubt I shall arrive at this end if I devote my attention sufficiently to those things which I perfectly understand; and if I separate from these that which I only understand confusedly and with obscurity. To these I shall henceforth diligently give heed.

MEDITATION V. *comes togethe*

Of the essence of material things, and, again, of God, that He exists.

Many other matters respecting the attributes of God and my own nature or mind remain for consideration; but I shall possibly on another occasion resume the investigation of these. Now (after first noting what must be done or avoided, in order to arrive at a knowledge of the truth) my principal task is to endeavour to emerge from the state of doubt into which I have these last days fallen, and to see whether nothing certain can be known regarding material things.

But before examining whether any such objects as I conceive exist outside of me, I must consider the ideas of them in so far as they are in my thought, and see which of them are distinct and which confused.

In the first place, I am able distinctly to imagine that quantity which philosophers commonly call continuous, or the extension in length, breadth, or depth, that is in this quantity, or rather in the object to which it is attributed. Further, I can number in it many different parts, and attribute to each of its parts many sorts of size, figure, situation and local movement, and, finally, I can assign to each of these movements all degrees of duration.

And not only do I know these things with distinctness when I consider them in general, but, likewise [however little I apply my attention to the matter], I discover an infinitude of particulars respecting numbers, figures, movements, and other such things, whose truth is so manifest, and so well accords with my nature, that when I begin to discover them, it seems to me that I learn nothing new, or recollect what I formerly knew—that is to say, that I for the first time perceive things which were already present to my mind, although I had not as yet applied my mind to them.

And what I here find to be most important is that I discover in myself an infinitude of ideas of certain things which cannot be esteemed as pure negations, although they may possibly have no existence outside of my thought, and which are not framed by me, although it is within my power either to think or not to think them, but which possess natures which are true and immutable. For example, when I imagine a triangle, although there may nowhere in the world be such a figure outside my thought, or ever have been, there is nevertheless in this figure a certain determinate nature, form, or essence, which is immutable and eternal, which I have not invented, and which in no wise depends on my mind, as appears from the fact that diverse properties of that triangle can be demonstrated, viz. that its three angles are equal to two right angles, that the greatest side is subtended by the greatest angle, and the like, which now, whether I wish it or do not wish it, I recognise very clearly as pertaining to it, although I never thought of the matter at all when I imagined a triangle for the first time, and which therefore cannot be said to have been invented by me.

Nor does the objection hold good that possibly this idea of a triangle has reached my mind through the medium of my senses, since I have sometimes seen bodies triangular in shape; because I can form in my mind an infinitude of other figures regarding which we cannot have the least conception of their ever having been objects of sense, and I can nevertheless demonstrate various properties pertaining to their nature as well as to that of the triangle, and these must certainly all be true since I conceive them clearly. Hence they are something, and not pure negation; for it is perfectly clear that all that is true is something, and I have already fully demonstrated that all that I know clearly is true. And even although I had not demonstrated this, the nature of my mind is such that I could not prevent myself from holding them to be true so long as I conceive them clearly; and I recollect that even when I was still strongly attached to the objects of sense, I counted as the most certain those truths which I conceived clearly as regards figures, numbers, and the other matters which pertain to arithmetic and geometry, and, in general, to pure and abstract mathematics.

But now, if just because I can draw the idea of something from my thought, it follows that all which I know clearly and distinctly as pertaining to this object does really belong to it, may I not derive from this an argument demonstrating the existence of God? It is certain that I no less find the idea of God, that is to say, the idea of a supremely perfect Being, in me, than that of any figure or number whatever it is; and I do not know any less clearly and distinctly that an [actual and] eternal existence pertains to this nature than I know that all that which I am able to demonstrate of some figure or number truly pertains to the nature of this figure or number, and therefore, although all that I concluded in the preceding Meditations were found to be false, the existence of God would pass with me as at least as certain as I have ever held the truths of mathematics (which concern only numbers and figures) to be.

This indeed is not at first manifest, since it would seem to present some appearance of being a sophism. For being accustomed in all other things to make a distinction between existence and essence, I easily persuade myself that the existence can be separated from the essence of God, and that we can thus conceive God as not actually existing. But, nevertheless, when I think of it with more attention, I clearly see that existence can no more be separated from the essence of God than can its having its three angles equal to two right angles be separated from the essence of a [rectilinear] triangle, or the idea of a mountain from the idea of a valley; and so there is not any less repugnance to our conceiving a God (that is, a Being supremely perfect) to whom existence is lacking (that is to say, to whom a certain perfection is lacking), than to conceive of a mountain which has no valley.

But although I cannot really conceive of a God without existence any more than a mountain without a valley, still from the fact that I conceive of a mountain with a valley, it does not follow that there is such a mountain in the world; similarly although I conceive of God as possessing existence, it would seem that it does not follow that there is a God which exists; for my thought does not impose any necessity upon things, and just as I may imagine a winged horse, although no horse with wings exists, so I could perhaps attribute existence to God, although no God existed.

But a sophism is concealed in this objection; for from the fact that I cannot conceive a mountain without a valley, it does not follow that there is any mountain or any valley in existence, but only that the mountain and the valley, whether they exist or do not exist, cannot in any way be separated one from the other. While from the fact that I cannot conceive God without existence, it follows that existence is inseparable from Him, and hence that He really exists; not that my thought can bring this to pass, or impose any necessity on things, but, on the contrary, because the necessity which lies in the thing itself, i.e. the necessity of the existence of God determines me to think in this way. For it is not within my power to think of God without existence (that is of a supremely perfect Being devoid of a supreme perfection) though it is in my power to imagine a horse either with wings or without wings.

And we must not here object that it is in truth necessary for me to assert that God exists after having presupposed that He possesses every sort of perfection, since existence is one of these, but that as a matter of fact my original supposition was not necessary, just as it is not necessary to consider that all quadrilateral figures can be inscribed in the circle; for supposing I thought this, I should be constrained to admit that the rhombus might be inscribed in the circle since it is a quadrilateral figure, which, however, is manifestly false. [We must not, I say, make any such allegations because] although it is not necessary that I should at any time entertain the notion of God, nevertheless whenever it happens that I think of a first and a sovereign Being, and, so to speak, derive the idea of Him from the storehouse of my mind, it is necessary that I should attribute to Him every sort of perfection, although I do not get so far as to enumerate them all, or to apply my mind to each one in particular. And this necessity suffices to make me conclude (after having recognised that existence is a perfection) that this first and sovereign Being really exists; just as though it is not necessary for me ever to imagine any triangle, yet, whenever I wish to consider a rectilinear figure composed only of three angles, it is absolutely essential that I should attribute to it all those properties which serve to bring about the conclusion that its three angles are not greater than two right angles, even although I may not then be considering this point in particular. But when I consider which figures are capable of being inscribed in the circle, it is in no wise necessary that I should think that all quadrilateral figures are of this number; on the contrary, I cannot even pretend that this is the case, so long as I do not desire to accept anything which I cannot conceive clearly and distinctly. And in consequence there is a great difference between the false suppositions such as this, and the true ideas born within me, the first and principal of which is that of God. For really I discern in many ways that this idea is not something factitious, and depending solely on my thought, but that it is the image of a true and immutable nature; first of all, because I cannot conceive anything but God himself to whose essence existence [necessarily] pertains; in the second place because it is not possible for me to conceive two or more Gods in this same position; and, granted that there is one such God who now exists,

I see clearly that it is necessary that He should have existed from all eternity, and that He must exist eternally; and finally, because I know an infinitude of other properties in God, none of which I can either diminish or change.

For the rest, whatever proof or argument I avail myself of, we must always return to the point that it is only those things which we conceive clearly and distinctly that have the power of persuading me entirely. And although amongst the matters which I conceive of in this way, some indeed are manifestly obvious to all, while others only manifest themselves to those who consider them closely and examine them attentively; still, after they have once been discovered, the latter are not esteemed as any less certain than the former. For example, in the case of every right-angled triangle, although it does not so manifestly appear that the square of the base is equal to the squares of the two other sides as that this base is opposite to the greatest angle; still, when this has once been apprehended, we are just as certain of its truth as of the truth of the other. And as regards God, if my mind were not pre-occupied with prejudices, and if my thought did not find itself on all hands diverted by the continual pressure of sensible things, there would be nothing which I could know more immediately and more easily than Him. For is there anything more manifest than that there is a God, that is to say, a Supreme Being, to whose essence alone existence pertains[1]?

And although for a firm grasp of this truth I have need of a strenuous application of mind, at present I not only feel myself to be as assured of it as of all that I hold as most certain, but I also remark that the certainty of all other things depends on it so absolutely, that without this knowledge it is impossible ever to know anything perfectly.

For although I am of such a nature that as long as[2] I understand anything very clearly and distinctly, I am naturally impelled to believe it to be true, yet because I am also of such a nature that I cannot have my mind constantly fixed on the same object in order to perceive it clearly, and as I often recollect having formed a past judgment without at the same time properly recollecting the reasons that led me to make it, it may happen meanwhile that other reasons present themselves to me, which would easily cause me to change my opinion, if I were ignorant of the facts of the existence

---

[1] 'In the idea of whom alone necessary or eternal existence is comprised.' French version.
[2] 'From the moment that.' French version.

of God, and thus I should have no true and certain knowledge, but only vague and vacillating opinions. Thus, for example, when I consider the nature of a [rectilinear] triangle, I who have some little knowledge of the principles of geometry recognise quite clearly that the three angles are equal to two right angles, and it is not possible for me not to believe this so long as I apply my mind to its demonstration; but so soon as I abstain from attending to the proof, although I still recollect having clearly comprehended it, it may easily occur that I come to doubt its truth, if I am ignorant of there being a God. For I can persuade myself of having been so constituted by nature that I can easily deceive myself even in those matters which I believe myself to apprehend with the greatest evidence and certainty, especially when I recollect that I have frequently judged matters to be true and certain which other reasons have afterwards impelled me to judge to be altogether false.

But after I have recognised that there is a God—because at the same time I have also recognised that all things depend upon Him, and that He is not a deceiver, and from that have inferred that what I perceive clearly and distinctly cannot fail to be true—although I no longer pay attention to the reasons for which I have judged this to be true, provided that I recollect having clearly and distinctly perceived it no contrary reason can be brought forward which could ever cause me to doubt of its truth; and thus I have a true and certain knowledge of it. And this same knowledge extends likewise to all other things which I recollect having formerly demonstrated, such as the truths of geometry and the like; for what can be alleged against them to cause me to place them in doubt? Will it be said that my nature is such as to cause me to be frequently deceived? But I already know that I cannot be deceived in the judgment whose grounds I know clearly. Will it be said that I formerly held many things to be true and certain which I have afterwards recognised to be false? But I had not had any clear and distinct knowledge of these things, and not as yet knowing the rule whereby I assure myself of the truth, I had been impelled to give my assent from reasons which I have since recognised to be less strong than I had at the time imagined them to be. What further objection can then be raised? That possibly I am dreaming (an objection I myself made a little while ago), or that all the thoughts which I now have are no more true than the phantasies of my dreams? But even though I slept the case would

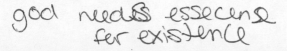
god needs essecene for existence

be the same, for all that is clearly present to my mind is absolutely
true.

And so I very clearly recognise that the certainty and truth of
all knowledge depends alone on the knowledge of the true God, in
so much that, before I knew Him, I could not have a perfect
knowledge of any other thing. And now that I know Him I have
the means of acquiring a perfect knowledge of an infinitude of
things, not only of those which relate to God Himself and other
intellectual matters, but also of those which pertain to corporeal
nature in so far as it is the object of pure mathematics [which have
no concern with whether it exists or not].

MEDITATION VI.

Of the Existence of Material Things, and of the real distinction between the Soul and Body of Man.

Nothing further now remains but to inquire whether material
things exist. And certainly I at least know that these may exist
in so far as they are considered as the objects of pure mathematics,
since in this aspect I perceive them clearly and distinctly. For there
is no doubt that God possesses the power to produce everything
that I am capable of perceiving with distinctness, and I have never
deemed that anything was impossible for Him, unless I found a
contradiction in attempting to conceive it clearly. Further, the
faculty of imagination which I possess, and of which, experience
tells me, I make use when I apply myself to the consideration of
material things, is capable of persuading me of their existence; for
when I attentively consider what imagination is, I find that it is
nothing but a certain application of the faculty of knowledge to the
body which is immediately present to it, and which therefore exists.

And to render this quite clear, I remark in the first place the
difference that exists between the imagination and pure intellection
[or conception[1]]. For example, when I imagine a triangle, I do not
conceive it only as a figure comprehended by three lines, but I also
apprehend[2] these three lines as present by the power and inward
vision of my mind[3], and this is what I call imagining. But if
I desire to think of a chiliagon, I certainly conceive truly that it is
a figure composed of a thousand sides, just as easily as I conceive

---

[1] 'Conception,' French version.   'intellectionem,' Latin version.
[2] intueor.   [3] acie mentis.

of a triangle that it is a figure of three sides only; but I cannot in any way imagine the thousand sides of a chiliagon [as I do the three sides of a triangle], nor do I, so to speak, regard them as present [with the eyes of my mind]. And although in accordance with the habit I have formed of always employing the aid of my imagination when I think of corporeal things, it may happen that in imagining a chiliagon I confusedly represent to myself some figure, yet it is very evident that this figure is not a chiliagon, since it in no way differs from that which I represent to myself when I think of a myriagon or any other many-sided figure; nor does it serve my purpose in discovering the properties which go to form the distinction between a chiliagon and other polygons. But if the question turns upon a pentagon, it is quite true that I can conceive its figure as well as that of a chiliagon without the help of my imagination; but I can also imagine it by applying the attention of my mind to each of its five sides, and at the same time to the space which they enclose. And thus I clearly recognise that I have need of a particular effort of mind in order to effect the act of imagination, such as I do not require in order to understand, and this particular effort of mind clearly manifests the difference which exists between imagination and pure intellection[1].

I remark besides that this power of imagination which is in one, inasmuch as it differs from the power of understanding, is in no wise a necessary element in my nature, or in [my essence, that is to say, in] the essence of my mind; for although I did not possess it I should doubtless ever remain the same as I now am, from which it appears that we might conclude that it depends on something which differs from me. And I easily conceive that if some body exists with which my mind is conjoined and united in such a way that it can apply itself to consider it when it pleases, it may be that by this means it can imagine corporeal objects; so that this mode of thinking differs from pure intellection only inasmuch as mind in its intellectual activity in some manner turns on itself, and considers some of the ideas which it possesses in itself; while in imagining it turns towards the body, and there beholds in it something conformable to the idea which it has either conceived of itself or perceived by the senses. I easily understand, I say, that the imagination could be thus constituted if it is true that body exists; and because I can discover no other

---

[1] intellectionem.

convenient mode of explaining it, I conjecture with probability that body does exist; but this is only with probability, and although I examine all things with care, I nevertheless do not find that from this distinct idea of corporeal nature, which I have in my imagination, I can derive any argument from which there will necessarily be deduced the existence of body.

But I am in the habit of imagining many other things besides this corporeal nature which is the object of pure mathematics, to wit, the colours, sounds, scents, pain, and other such things, although less distinctly. And inasmuch as I perceive these things much better through the senses, by the medium of which, and by the memory, they seem to have reached my imagination, I believe that, in order to examine them more conveniently, it is right that I should at the same time investigate the nature of sense perception, and that I should see if from the ideas which I apprehend by this mode of thought, which I call feeling, I cannot derive some certain proof of the existence of corporeal objects.

And first of all I shall recall to my memory those matters which I hitherto held to be true, as having perceived them through the senses, and the foundations on which my belief has rested; in the next place I shall examine the reasons which have since obliged me to place them in doubt; in the last place I shall consider which of them I must now believe.

First of all, then, I perceived that I had a head, hands, feet, and all other members of which this body—which I considered as a part, or possibly even as the whole, of myself—is composed. Further I was sensible that this body was placed amidst many others, from which it was capable of being affected in many different ways, beneficial and hurtful, and I remarked that a certain feeling of pleasure accompanied those that were beneficial, and pain those which were harmful. And in addition to this pleasure and pain, I also experienced hunger, thirst, and other similar appetites, as also certain corporeal inclinations towards joy, sadness, anger, and other similar passions. And outside myself, in addition to extension, figure, and motions of bodies, I remarked in them hardness, heat, and all other tactile qualities, and, further, light and colour, and scents and sounds, the variety of which gave me the means of distinguishing the sky, the earth, the sea, and generally all the other bodies, one from the other. And certainly, considering the ideas of all these qualities which presented themselves to my mind, and which alone I perceived properly or immediately, it was not without reason that I believed myself to perceive objects quite different from my thought, to wit, bodies from which those ideas proceeded; for I found by experience that these ideas presented themselves to me without my consent being requisite, so that I could not perceive any object, however desirous I might be, unless it were present to the organs of sense; and it was not in my power not to perceive it, when it was present. And because the ideas which I received through the senses were much more lively, more clear, and even, in their own way, more distinct than any of those which I could of myself frame in meditation, or than those I found impressed on my memory, it appeared as though they could not have proceeded from my mind, so that they must necessarily have been produced in me by some other things. And having no knowledge of those objects excepting the knowledge which the ideas themselves gave me, nothing was more likely to occur to my mind than that the objects were similar to the ideas which were caused. And because I likewise remembered that I had formerly made use of my senses rather than my reason, and recognised that the ideas which I formed of myself were not so distinct as those which I perceived through the senses, and that they were most frequently even composed of portions of these last, I persuaded myself easily that I had no idea in my mind which had not formerly come to me through the senses. Nor was it without some reason that I believed that this body (which by a certain special right I call my own) belonged to me more properly and more strictly than any other; for in fact I could never be separated from it as from other bodies; I experienced in it and on account of it all my appetites and affections, and finally I was touched by the feeling of pain and the titillation of pleasure in its parts, and not in the parts of other bodies which were separated from it. But when I inquired, why, from some, I know not what, painful sensation, there follows sadness of mind, and from the pleasurable sensation there arises joy, or why this mysterious pinching of the stomach which I call hunger causes me to desire to eat, and dryness of throat causes a desire to drink, and so on, I could give no reason excepting that nature taught me so; for there is certainly no affinity (that I at least can understand) between the craving of the stomach and the desire to eat, any more than between the perception of whatever causes pain and the thought of sadness which arises from this perception. And in the same way it appeared to me that I had learned from nature all the other judgments which I formed regarding the objects of my senses, since I remarked that these judgments were formed in me before I had the leisure to weigh and consider any reasons which might oblige me to make them.

But afterwards many experiences little by little destroyed all the faith which I had rested in my senses; for I from time to time observed that those towers which from afar appeared to me to be round, more closely observed seemed square, and that colossal statues raised on the summit of these towers, appeared as quite tiny statues when viewed from the bottom; and so in an infinitude of other cases I found error in judgments founded on the external senses. And not only in those founded on the external senses, but even in those founded on the internal as well; for is there anything more intimate or more internal than pain? And yet I have learned from some persons whose arms or legs have been cut off, that they sometimes seemed to feel pain in the part which had been amputated, which made me think that I could not be quite certain that it was a certain member which pained me, even although I felt pain in it. And to those grounds of doubt I have lately added two others, which are very general; the first is that I never have believed myself to feel anything in waking moments which I cannot also sometimes believe myself to feel when I sleep, and as I do not think that these things which I seem to feel in sleep, proceed from objects outside of me, I do not see any reason why I should have this belief regarding objects which I seem to perceive while awake. The other was that being still ignorant, or rather supposing myself to be ignorant, of the author of my being, I saw nothing to prevent me from having been so constituted by nature that I might be deceived even in matters which seemed to me to be most certain. And as to the grounds on which I was formerly persuaded of the truth of sensible objects, I had not much trouble in replying to them. For since nature seemed to cause me to lean towards many things from which reason repelled me, I did not believe that I should trust much to the teachings of nature. And although the ideas which I receive by the senses do not depend on my will, I did not think that one should for that reason conclude that they proceeded from things different from myself, since possibly some faculty might be discovered in me—though hitherto unknown to me—which produced them.

But now that I begin to know myself better, and to discover more clearly the author of my being, I do not in truth think that I should rashly admit all the matters which the senses seem to teach us, but, on the other hand, I do not think that I should doubt them all universally.

And first of all, because I know that all things which I apprehend clearly and distinctly can be created by God as I apprehend them, it suffices that I am able to apprehend one thing apart from another clearly and distinctly in order to be certain that the one is different from the other, since they may be made to exist in separation at least by the omnipotence of God ; and it does not signify by what power this separation is made in order to compel me to judge them to be different : and, therefore, just because I know certainly that I exist, and that meanwhile I do not remark that any other thing necessarily pertains to my nature or essence, excepting that I am a thinking thing, I rightly conclude that my essence consists solely in the fact that I am a thinking thing [or a substance whose whole essence or nature is to think]. And although possibly (or rather certainly, as I shall say in a moment) I possess a body with which I am very intimately conjoined, yet because, on the one side, I have a clear and distinct idea of myself inasmuch as I am only a thinking and unextended thing, and as, on the other, I possess a distinct idea of body, inasmuch as it is only an extended and unthinking thing, it is certain that this I [that is to say, my soul by which I am what I am], is entirely and absolutely distinct from my body, and can exist without it.

I further find in myself faculties employing modes of thinking peculiar to themselves, to wit, the faculties of imagination and feeling, without which I can easily conceive myself clearly and distinctly as a complete being ; while, on the other hand, they cannot be so conceived apart from me, that is without an intelligent substance in which they reside, for [in the notion we have of these faculties, or, to use the language of the Schools] in their formal concept, some kind of intellection is comprised, from which I infer that they are distinct from me as its modes are from a thing. I observe also in me some other faculties such as that of change of position, the assumption of different figures and such like, which cannot be conceived, any more than can the preceding, apart from some substance to which they are attached, and consequently cannot exist without it ; but it is very clear that these faculties, if it be true that they exist, must be attached to some corporeal or extended substance, and not to an intelligent substance, since in the clear and distinct conception of these there is some sort of extension found to be present, but no intellection at all.

There is certainly further in me a certain passive faculty of perception, that is, of receiving and recognising the ideas of sensible things, but this would be useless to me [and I could in no way avail myself of it], if there were not either in me or in some other thing another active faculty capable of forming and producing these ideas. But this active faculty cannot exist in me [inasmuch as I am a thing that thinks] seeing that it does not presuppose thought, and also that those ideas are often produced in me without my contributing in any way to the same, and often even against my will; it is thus necessarily the case that the faculty resides in some substance different from me in which all the reality which is objectively in the ideas that are produced by this faculty is formally or eminently contained, as I remarked before. And this substance is either a body, that is, a corporeal nature in which there is contained formally [and really] all that which is objectively [and by representation] in those ideas, or it is God Himself, or some other creature more noble than body in which that same is contained eminently. But, since God is no deceiver, it is very manifest that He does not communicate to me these ideas immediately and by Himself, nor yet by the intervention of some creature in which their reality is not formally, but only eminently, contained. For since He has given me no faculty to recognise that this is the case, but, on the other hand, a very great inclination to believe [that they are sent to me or] that they are conveyed to me by corporeal objects, I do not see how He could be defended from the accusation of deceit if these ideas were produced by causes other than corporeal objects. Hence we must allow that corporeal things exist. However, they are perhaps not exactly what we perceive by the senses, since this comprehension by the senses is in many instances very obscure and confused; but we must at least admit that all things which I conceive in them clearly and distinctly, that is to say, all things which, speaking generally, are comprehended in the object of pure mathematics, are truly to be recognised as external objects.

As to other things, however, which are either particular only, as, for example, that the sun is of such and such a figure, etc., or which are less clearly and distinctly conceived, such as light, sound, pain and the like, it is certain that although they are very dubious and uncertain, yet on the sole ground that God is not a deceiver, and that consequently He has not permitted any falsity to exist in my opinion which He has not likewise given me the faculty of correcting, I may assuredly hope to conclude that I have within me the means of arriving at the truth even here. And first of all there is no doubt that in all things which nature teaches me there is some truth contained; for by nature, considered in general, I now understand no other thing than either God Himself or else the order and disposition which God has established in created things; and by my nature in particular I understand no other thing than the complexus of all the things which God has given me.

But there is nothing which this nature teaches me more expressly [nor more sensibly] than that I have a body which is adversely affected when I feel pain, which has need of food or drink when I experience the feelings of hunger and thirst, and so on; nor can I doubt there being some truth in all this.

Nature also teaches me by these sensations of pain, hunger, thirst, etc., that I am not only lodged in my body as a pilot in a vessel, but that I am very closely united to it, and so to speak so intermingled with it that I seem to compose with it one whole. For if that were not the case, when my body is hurt, I, who am merely a thinking thing, should not feel pain, for I should perceive this wound by the understanding only, just as the sailor perceives by sight when something is damaged in his vessel; and when my body has need of drink or food, I should clearly understand the fact without being warned of it by confused feelings of hunger and thirst. For all these sensations of hunger, thirst, pain, etc. are in truth none other than certain confused modes of thought which are produced by the union and apparent intermingling of mind and body.

Moreover, nature teaches me that many other bodies exist around mine, of which some are to be avoided, and others sought after. And certainly from the fact that I am sensible of different sorts of colours, sounds, scents, tastes, heat, hardness, etc., I very easily conclude that there are in the bodies from which all these diverse sense-perceptions proceed certain variations which answer to them, although possibly these are not really at all similar to them. And also from the fact that amongst these different sense-perceptions some are very agreeable to me and others disagreeable, it is quite certain that my body (or rather myself in my entirety, inasmuch as I am formed of body and soul) may receive different impressions agreeable and disagreeable from the other bodies which surround it.

But there are many other things which nature seems to have taught me, but which at the same time I have never really received from her, but which have been brought about in my mind by a certain habit which I have of forming inconsiderate judgments on things; and thus it may easily happen that these judgments contain some error. Take, for example, the opinion which I hold that all space in which there is nothing that affects [or makes an impression on] my senses is void; that in a body which is warm there is something entirely similar to the idea of heat which is in me; that in a white or green body there is the same whiteness or greenness that I perceive; that in a bitter or sweet body there is the same taste, and so on in other instances; that the stars, the towers, and all other distant bodies are of the same figure and size as they appear from far off to our eyes, etc. But in order that in this there should be nothing which I do not conceive distinctly, I should define exactly what I really understand when I say that I am taught somewhat by nature. For here I take nature in a more limited signification than when I term it the sum of all the things given me by God, since in this sum many things are comprehended which only pertain to mind (and to these I do not refer in speaking of nature) such as the notion which I have of the fact that what has once been done cannot ever be undone and an infinitude of such things which I know by the light of nature [without the help of the body]; and seeing that it comprehends many other matters besides which only pertain to body, and are no longer here contained under the name of nature, such as the quality of weight which it possesses and the like, with which I also do not deal; for in talking of nature I only treat of those things given by God to me as a being composed of mind and body. But the nature here described truly teaches me to flee from things which cause the sensation of pain, and seek after the things which communicate to me the sentiment of pleasure and so forth; but I do not see that beyond this it teaches me that from those diverse sense-perceptions we should ever form any conclusion regarding things outside of us, without having [carefully and maturely] mentally examined them beforehand. For it seems to me that it is mind alone, and not mind and body in conjunction, that is requisite to a knowledge of the truth in regard to such things. Thus, although a star makes no larger an impression on my eye than the flame of a little candle there is yet in me no real or positive propensity impelling me to believe that it is not greater than that flame; but I have judged it to be so from my earliest years, without any rational foundation. And although in approaching fire I feel heat, and in approaching it a little too near I even feel pain, there is at the same time no reason in this which could persuade me that there is in the fire something resembling this heat any more than there is in it something resembling the pain; all that I have any reason to believe from this is, that there is something in it, whatever it may be, which excites in me these sensations of heat or of pain. So also, although there are spaces in which I find nothing which excites my senses, I must not from that conclude that these spaces contain no body; for I see in this, as in other similar things, that I have been in the habit of perverting the order of nature, because these perceptions of sense having been placed within me by nature merely for the purpose of signifying to my mind what things are beneficial or hurtful to the composite whole of which it forms a part, and being up to that point sufficiently clear and distinct, I yet avail myself of them as though they were absolute rules by which I might immediately determine the essence of the bodies which are outside me, as to which, in fact, they can teach me nothing but what is most obscure and confused.

But I have already sufficiently considered how, notwithstanding the supreme goodness of God, falsity enters into the judgments I make. Only here a new difficulty is presented—one respecting those things the pursuit or avoidance of which is taught me by nature, and also respecting the internal sensations which I possess, and in which I seem to have sometimes detected error [and thus to be directly deceived by my own nature]. To take an example, the agreeable taste of some food in which poison has been intermingled may induce me to partake of the poison, and thus deceive me. It is true, at the same time, that in this case nature may be excused, for it only induces me to desire food in which I find a pleasant taste, and not to desire the poison which is unknown to it; and thus I can infer nothing from this fact, except that my nature is not omniscient, at which there is certainly no reason to be astonished, since man, being finite in nature, can only have knowledge the perfectness of which is limited.

But we not unfrequently deceive ourselves even in those things to which we are directly impelled by nature, as happens with those who when they are sick desire to drink or eat things hurtful to them. It will perhaps be said here that the cause of their deceptiveness is that their nature is corrupt, but that does not remove the difficulty, because a sick man is none the less truly God's creature than he who is in health; and it is therefore as repugnant to God's

goodness for the one to have a deceitful nature as it is for the other.
And as a clock composed of wheels and counter-weights no less
exactly observes the laws of nature when it is badly made, and
does not show the time properly, than when it entirely satisfies the
wishes of its maker, and as, if I consider the body of a man as
being a sort of machine so built up and composed of nerves, muscles,
veins, blood and skin, that though there were no mind in it at all,
it would not cease to have the same motions as at present, exception
being made of those movements which are due to the direction of
the will, and in consequence depend upon the mind [as opposed to
those which operate by the disposition of its organs], I easily
recognise that it would be as natural to this body, supposing it to
be, for example, dropsical, to suffer the parchedness of the throat
which usually signifies to the mind the feeling of thirst, and to be
disposed by this parched feeling to move the nerves and other parts
in the way requisite for drinking, and thus to augment its malady
and do harm to itself, as it is natural to it, when it has no indis-
position, to be impelled to drink for its good by a similar cause.
And although, considering the use to which the clock has been
destined by its maker, I may say that it deflects from the order of
its nature when it does not indicate the hours correctly; and as, in
the same way, considering the machine of the human body as
having been formed by God in order to have in itself all the movements usually manifested there, I have reason for thinking that it
does not follow the order of nature when, if the throat is dry,
drinking does harm to the conservation of health, nevertheless I
recognise at the same time that this last mode of explaining nature
is very different from the other. For this is but a purely verbal
characterisation depending entirely on my thought, which compares
a sick man and a badly constructed clock with the idea which
I have of a healthy man and a well made clock, and it is hence
extrinsic to the things to which it is applied ; but according to the
other interpretation of the term nature I understand something
which is truly found in things and which is therefore not without
some truth.

But certainly although in regard to the dropsical body it is only
so to speak to apply an extrinsic term when we say that its nature is
corrupted, inasmuch as apart from the need to drink, the throat
is parched ; yet in regard to the composite whole, that is to say, to
the mind or soul united to this body, it is not a purely verbal
predicate, but a real error of nature, for it to have thirst when

drinking would be hurtful to it. And thus it still remains to inquire how the goodness of God does not prevent the nature of man so regarded from being fallacious.

In order to begin this examination, then, I here say, in the first place, that there is a great difference between mind and body, inasmuch as body is by nature always divisible, and the mind is entirely indivisible. For, as a matter of fact, when I consider the mind, that is to say, myself inasmuch as I am only a thinking thing, I cannot distinguish in myself any parts, but apprehend myself to be clearly one and entire; and although the whole mind seems to be united to the whole body, yet if a foot, or an arm, or some other part, is separated from my body, I am aware that nothing has been taken away from my mind. And the faculties of willing, feeling, conceiving, etc. cannot be properly speaking said to be its parts, for it is one and the same mind which employs itself in willing and in feeling and understanding. But it is quite otherwise with corporeal or extended objects, for there is not one of these imaginable by me which my mind cannot easily divide into parts, and which consequently I do not recognise as being divisible; this would be sufficient to teach me that the mind or soul of man is entirely different from the body, if I had not already learned it from other sources.

I further notice that the mind does not receive the impressions from all parts of the body immediately, but only from the brain, or perhaps even from one of its smallest parts, to wit, from that in which the common sense[1] is said to reside, which, whenever it is disposed in the same particular way, conveys the same thing to the mind, although meanwhile the other portions of the body may be differently disposed, as is testified by innumerable experiments which it is unnecessary here to recount.

I notice, also, that the nature of body is such that none of its parts can be moved by another part a little way off which cannot also be moved in the same way by each one of the parts which are between the two, although this more remote part does not act at all. As, for example, in the cord *ABCD* [which is in tension] if we pull the last part *D*, the first part *A* will not be moved in any way differently from what would be the case if one of the intervening parts *B* or *C* were pulled, and the last part *D* were to remain unmoved. And in the same way, when I feel pain in my foot, my knowledge of physics teaches me that this sensation is communicated by means of nerves dispersed through the foot, which, being

[1] sensus communis.

extended like cords from there to the brain, when they are contracted
in the foot, at the same time contract the inmost portions of the
brain which is their extremity and place of origin, and then excite
a certain movement which nature has established in order to cause
the mind to be affected by a sensation of pain represented as existing
in the foot.   But because these nerves must pass through the tibia,
the thigh, the loins, the back and the neck, in order to reach from
the leg to the brain, it may happen that although their extremities
which are in the foot are not affected, but only certain ones of their
intervening parts [which pass by the loins or the neck], this action
will excite the same movement in the brain that might have been
excited there by a hurt received in the foot, in consequence of
which the mind will necessarily feel in the foot the same pain as if
it had received a hurt.   And the same holds good of all the other
perceptions of our senses.

I notice finally that since each of the movements which are in
the portion of the brain by which the mind is immediately affected
brings about one particular sensation only, we cannot under the circumstances imagine anything more likely than that this movement,
amongst all the sensations which it is capable of impressing on it,
causes mind to be affected by that one which is best fitted and
most generally useful for the conservation of the human body when
it is in health.   But experience makes us aware that all the feelings
with which nature inspires us are such as I have just spoken of;
and there is therefore nothing in them which does not give testimony
to the power and goodness of the God [who has produced them[1]].
Thus, for example, when the nerves which are in the feet are
violently or more than usually moved, their movement, passing
through the medulla of the spine[2] to the inmost parts of the brain,
gives a sign to the mind which makes it feel somewhat, to wit, pain,
as though in the foot, by which the mind is excited to do its utmost
to remove the cause of the evil as dangerous and hurtful to the
foot.   It is true that God could have constituted the nature of man
in such a way that this same movement in the brain would have
conveyed something quite different to the mind; for example, it
might have produced consciousness of itself either in so far as it is
in the brain, or as it is in the foot, or as it is in some other place
between the foot and the brain, or it might finally have produced
consciousness of anything else whatsoever; but none of all this would
have contributed so well to the conservation of the body.   Similarly,

[1] Latin version only.   [2] spini dorsae medullam.

when we desire to drink, a certain dryness of the throat is produced which moves its nerves, and by their means the internal portions of the brain; and this movement causes in the mind the sensation of thirst, because in this case there is nothing more useful to us than to become aware that we have need to drink for the conservation of our health; and the same holds good in other instances.

From this it is quite clear that, notwithstanding the supreme goodness of God, the nature of man, inasmuch as it is composed of mind and body, cannot be otherwise than sometimes a source of deception. For if there is any cause which excites, not in the foot but in some part of the nerves which are extended between the foot and the brain, or even in the brain itself, the same movement which usually is produced when the foot is detrimentally affected, pain will be experienced as though it were in the foot, and the sense will thus naturally be deceived; for since the same movement in the brain is capable of causing but one sensation in the mind, and this sensation is much more frequently excited by a cause which hurts the foot than by another existing in some other quarter, it is reasonable that it should convey to the mind pain in the foot rather than in any other part of the body. And although the parchedness of the throat does not always proceed, as it usually does, from the fact that drinking is necessary for the health of the body, but sometimes comes from quite a different cause, as is the case with dropsical patients, it is yet much better that it should mislead on this occasion than if, on the other hand, it were always to deceive us when the body is in good health; and so on in similar cases.

And certainly this consideration is of great service to me, not only in enabling me to recognise all the errors to which my nature is subject, but also in enabling me to avoid them or to correct them more easily. For knowing that all my senses more frequently indicate to me truth than falsehood respecting the things which concern that which is beneficial to the body, and being able almost always to avail myself of many of them in order to examine one particular thing, and, besides that, being able to make use of my memory in order to connect the present with the past, and of my understanding which already has discovered all the causes of my errors, I ought no longer to fear that falsity may be found in matters every day presented to me by my senses. And I ought to set aside all the doubts of these past days as hyperbolical and ridiculous, particularly that very common uncertainty respecting sleep, which I could not distinguish from the waking state ; for at present I find a very notable difference between the two, inasmuch as our memory can never connect our dreams one with the other, or with the whole course of our lives, as it unites events which happen to us while we are awake.   And, as a matter of fact, if someone, while I was awake, quite suddenly appeared to me and disappeared as fast as do the images which I see in sleep, so that I could not know from whence the form came nor whither it went, it would not be without reason that I should deem it a spectre or a phantom formed by my brain [and similar to those which I form in sleep], rather than a real man.   But when I perceive things as to which I know distinctly both the place from which they proceed, and that in which they are, and the time at which they appeared to me ; and when, without any interruption, I can connect the perceptions which I have of them with the whole course of my life, I am perfectly assured that these perceptions occur while I am waking and not during sleep.   And I ought in no wise to doubt the truth of such matters, if, after having called up all my senses, my memory, and my understanding, to examine them, nothing is brought to evidence by any one of them which is repugnant to what is set forth by the others.   For because God is in no wise a deceiver, it follows that I am not deceived in this.   But because the exigencies of action often oblige us to make up our minds before having leisure to examine matters carefully, we must confess that the life of man is very frequently subject to error in respect to individual objects, and we must in the end acknowledge the infirmity of our nature.

power of senses → outside of him

mind
←
-thinking
-consciousness
-perception

Brain
-organ

Soul

Body

what is consciousness?
- self aware
- thought
- concept of time

western -christian idea
    body is tied to sin, imperfect
    soul is heavenly, perfect

All dualism, splits all the
way through our lives.